THE JOY OF FULL SURRENDER

PARACLETE ESSENTIALS

The Joy of Full Surrender

JEAN-PIERRE DE CAUSSADE
Foreword by Michael Casey, ocso

A REVISED TRANSLATION
of THE FRENCH CLASSIC
L'ABANDON À LA PROVIDENCE DIVINE

EDITED BY HAL M. HELMS AND ROBERT J. EDMONSON, cj

PARACLETE PRESS
BREWSTER, MASSACHUSETTS

The Joy of Full Surrender

2008 First Printing

Copyright © 2008 by Paraclete Press, Inc.

ISBN: 978-1-55725-609-6

Library of Congress Cataloging-in-Publication Data

Caussade, Jean Pierre de, d. 1751.
  [Abandon à la providence divine. English]
  The joy of full surrender / by Jean-Pierre De Caussade.
    p. cm.
  ISBN 978-1-55725-609-6
  1. Mysticism—Catholic Church. 2. Spiritual life—Catholic Church. I.
Title.
  BV5082.3.C3813 2008b
  248.2'2--dc22   2008039112

10 9 8 7 6 5 4 3 2 1

Published by Paraclete Press
Brewster, Massachusetts
www.paracletepress.com

Printed in the United States of America

CONTENTS

BOOK II
THE STATE OF BEING SURRENDERED
TO GOD'S WILL

BOOK III
GOD'S FATHERLY CARE OF
THOSE WHO PRACTICE SELF-SURRENDER

S OME THIRTY YEARS AGO flying from point to point in Papua New Guinea, I found myself sitting in the copilot's seat. As we buckled ourselves in, the pilot looked over at me and said laconically, "Don't touch anything." As we traversed the vast ocean of jungle green more than a mile below us, I sat like a rock with my hands on my knees, trying not to be alarmed by the flashing lights and flickering gauges, and making sure not to bump into any of the controls that were so close at hand, directly in front of me. Understanding nothing. Despite or because of my total inability to contribute anything, we arrived at our destination without incident.

This experience has been a metaphor for me of an imperative of the spiritual life. I—we—encounter these sorts of situations from time to time in the course of our journeys. We are compelled to yield complete control into the hands of God so that the divine will can work its saving wonder in us. At times like these, God's word to us is, "Don't touch anything."

I count myself blessed that, at an important juncture in my life, a wise elder introduced me to the writings of Caussade. From them I gained not only the guidance I needed to traverse a difficult terrain, but also a permanent element in my outlook on life: an appreciation of the operation of God's providence and my need to be receptive of that providence despite the lack of full understanding and the pressure of contrary desires.

The original title of Caussade's work was *Abandonment to Divine Providence*, and it is in this notion of "self-surrender" (as it is translated in the present version) that the book finds its focus. For Caussade, holiness consisted in faithfulness to God's will, however this be manifested. The greatest obstacles to this conformity are our delusions that disguise the promptings of self-will and set us in opposition to God's working in our life. We fail to understand that everything that happens in and around us needs to be interpreted as part of God's lifelong conversation with us. This means that every opportunity for action that presents itself is an invitation from God to draw closer, every burden we experience can be a means of growth, whatever suffering comes our way is a divinely chosen means of bringing us to joy and holiness.

Caussade uses the phrase "the sacrament of the present moment" to make the point that at every moment of every day we have the opportunity to do God's will as best we know it. Making this intention a priority in life is a sure means to deep inner peace, just as resistance to God's will—conscious or unconscious—is a certain source of agitation, fault-finding, and confusion.

Caussade is often categorized as belonging to the so-called Quietist movement. But, in reality, his doctrine has two interrelating parts. Alongside the passive acceptance of whatever life brings, there is an emphasis on the wholehearted performance of whatever duties are attached to one's state in life. In fact, this active fulfilment of God's will is given primacy. "It is foolish to envisage any kind of self-surrender in which all personal activity is excluded," he explains.

And what precisely is "self-surrender"? It involves the kind of faith or trust that acts on conviction that nothing can separate us from the love of Christ. The only things that can truly stand in our way are our own compulsions to mastermind our lives and our own failures to yield control into the hands of Another.

—*Michael Casey*

ABOUT THIS EDITION

This is a revised English translation, using as the main sources from which to work a very fine English version by E.J. Strickland, published in England in 1921, and an older but incomplete version by Ella McMahon, published by Benziger Brothers in 1887. We have referred to all other English versions available for the sake of clarifying some of the difficult passages, and compared it with the eighth French edition. For this new edition, the original 1986 edition has been reviewed in its entirety and further modernized.

INTRODUCTION

WHEN *ABANDONMENT TO DIVINE PROVIDENCE* was first presented to the Christian public in France in 1861, it became an immediate hit. A classic work of spirituality, it has gone through many editions, some of which included additional letters written by the author. Under the same name it has been translated into several foreign languages. *The Joy of Full Surrender* is a newly edited version of this classic work, following the eighth French edition. It consists of collected notes from retreats and talks that had been given to several communities of religious by the Rev. Jean-Pierre de Caussade, sj, who died in 1751. These notes were carefully kept and transmitted within these communities because of the high value attached to them. Caussade has been credited with playing an important part in the spiritual renewal among French Catholics of the nineteenth century, not only because of his respected preaching, but also because of his letters and other writings.

Fr. Henri Ramire arranged these notes in their present order, adding whatever connecting thoughts and explanations he thought necessary to make them useful for people seeking the joy of full surrender to God. His version has been termed "a veritable mosaic" made up of Caussade's own words and those of Ramire himself. Nonetheless, it is this format in which the book has been widely read and loved, and we have thought it worthwhile to bring out another edition of it in today's English.

Ramire set forth three principles to guide the reader in meditating on these pages, two of them from Caussade, and one from himself. They are as follows:

First principle: "Nothing is done, nothing happens, either in the material or in the moral world, that God has not foreseen from all eternity, and that he has not willed, or at least permitted."

Second principle: "God can will nothing, he can permit nothing, but in view of the end he proposed to himself in creating the world; that is, in view of his glory and the glory of Jesus Christ, his only Son."

Third principle: "As long as human beings live upon earth, God desires to be glorified through the happiness of these privileged creatures; and consequently in God's designs the interest of making human beings holy and happy is inseparable from the interest of the divine glory."

It is important to emphasize that Caussade never intends to lead his hearers into a passive fatalism. Nothing could be farther from his intent. The surrender called for here is the *Yet not what I want but what you want* of our blessed Lord, and the *Let it be with me according to your word* of his blessed mother.

Dom David Knowles, in his introduction to an earlier edition of this work, says, "If we set ourselves to choose the ten greatest spiritual guides since St. Bernard—a magnificent list, indeed, including St. Teresa, St. John of the Cross and St. Francis of Sales—it would without a doubt be necessary to find a place for Father de Caussade."

Perhaps a word needs to be said about the change of title and the problem of translating Caussade's French word *abandon* into some English equivalent. The word *abandonment* today has a negative connotation, hardly compatible with the central thrust of Caussade's thought. Some writers have used the word "self-abandonment" to try to convey the thought more accurately.

If one sentence could characterize this book above all others, it would be this: "God's will is always good, no matter how it may appear at the moment."

It may be argued that the teachings of this book are more suitable to those living in enclosed communities of contemplative monks and nuns, such as those to whom many of its words were first addressed. But it may also be seen from Caussade's own words, that the truths here and the call here are for all who love our Lord Jesus Christ with a simple and childlike faith. Whatever our state of life, there is always a "beyond" to our present level of commitment and surrender. And it is to the souls who feel the drawing of his great love to that fuller surrender of themselves to God that these words are addressed.

It is our prayer that such souls will find this book a welcome help on the path that leads to a closer walk with God.

BOOK I

WHY FULL SURRENDER?

CHAPTER 1

Holiness Means Faithfulness to God's Will

God speaks today in the same way he spoke to our ancestors. There were no spiritual directors then, and spiritual methods were not so clearly defined. Spirituality simply consisted of faithfulness to the will of God. It was not reduced to an art, minutely explained, containing so many directions, maxims, or instructions as there are today. Our present needs may require this, but in those earlier days, when God's people were more simple and upright, it was enough to see that each moment brought a duty to be faithfully fulfilled. Their whole attention was fixed on that duty, like the hour hand of a clock that moves its necessary distance minute by minute. With their mind and spirit constantly moved by the impulse of the Spirit, they turned imperceptibly to each new task that God presented to them at each hour of the day.

Such were the secret springs of Mary's life, the most perfect example of simple and absolute surrender to the will of God. Her reply to the angel, "Let it be with me according to your word" (Luke 1:38), expressed all the mystical teaching of her ancestors. All that theology was reduced, as it still is today, to the purest, simplest surrender of a soul to the will of God in whatever form his will might present itself. This beautiful and noble attitude, the very essence of Mary's spirituality, is brilliantly shown in the words "Let it be with me." Notice how perfectly those words match the words our Lord would have always on our lips and in our hearts: "Yet not what I want but what you want." It is true that what was required of Mary at that moment was indeed something glorious for her. But all the splendor of that glory would have made no impression on her if she had not seen in it the fulfillment of God's will.

It was God's will alone that mattered to her. Whatever her occupations, commonplace or extraordinary, they were to her eyes only appearances, sometimes obscure, sometimes clear, within which she could worship God and recognize the workings of his almighty hand. She joyfully accepted the duty or suffering that each moment brought as a gift from him who fills with good things the hearts of those who hunger and thirst for him alone and have no desire for created things or empty fantasies.

CHAPTER 2

Shadows That Veil the Hand of God

The power of the Most High will overshadow you, said the angel to Mary. This shadow, behind which is hidden the power of God for the purpose of bringing forth Jesus Christ in the soul, is the duty, the attraction, or the cross that is offered to us at each moment. These are, in truth, only shadows like those in nature that, like a veil, cover the objects of our senses and hide them from us. In the same way, in the moral and supernatural realm, the duties of each moment, like dark shadows, conceal the only thing that should hold our attention: the reality of God's will in them. This was the way Mary perceived them. As these shadows spread themselves over her mind, far from deluding her, they only increased her faith in the One who is unchanging and unchangeable. Withdraw, Archangel! You are only a shadow.

Your moment has passed. You have delivered your message and you are gone. Mary passes beyond you without stopping. The Holy Spirit, with whom she has been filled under the outward appearance of your words, will never leave her.

There are remarkably few extraordinary events in the exterior life of the most holy Virgin. At least there are none recorded in Holy Scripture. Her life is pictured as outwardly very ordinary and simple. She did what others in a similar state of life might do, and suffered what they might suffer. She went to visit her cousin Elizabeth. Other relatives do that, too. She took shelter in a stable as a result of her poverty. She returned to Nazareth, from which she had been driven by the persecution of Herod, and lived there with Jesus and Joseph, who supported themselves by the work of their hands.

Such was the daily bread of the holy family. But what a divine nourishment Mary and Joseph received from this daily bread for the strengthening of their faith! It was like a sacrament to make all their moments holy! What treasures of grace lay concealed in these moments under the guise of the most commonplace events. That which was visible might happen to anyone, but the invisible, when understood and discerned by faith, was no less than God himself working great things. Bread of angels! Heavenly manna! Pearl of great value! Sacrament of the present moment! You bring God under the poor and humble appearance of the manger, the hay, and the straw! But to whom do you give him? "He has filled the hungry with good things" (Luke 1:53). God reveals himself to the humble in the lowliest things; but the proud, who attach importance only to outward appearances, cannot find him even in great things and are sent away empty.

CHAPTER 3
The Work of Making Us Holy

If the work of making us holy seems such a hard and impossible task, it is because we do not have the right idea of what it truly is. In truth, holiness consists of one single thing: faithfulness to the will of God. Now, this faithfulness is within the reach of everyone, whether it calls for active or passive practice of our faith.

Active faithfulness means fulfilling the duties that are ours by the general laws of God and of the Church, or by our particular state of life. Passive faithfulness consists in the loving acceptance of all that God sends us each moment.

Is either of these practices beyond our ability? Not active faithfulness, because any duties it might impose are no longer duties when we do not have the power to fulfill them. If the state of your health does not permit you to attend church, you are not obliged to go. The same rule holds good for all the precepts that have to do with duties to fulfill. Only those that forbid things that are evil in themselves are absolute, because it is never allowable to commit sin. Can anything, then, be easier or more reasonable? What excuse can we offer? Yet this is all that God requires of the soul for the work of making us holy. God requires it of both the rich and the poor, the strong and the weak—in a word, of everyone, always and everywhere.

So it is true that God requires nothing from us but what is simple and easy, for this simple method is sufficient to enable us to attain an eminent degree of holiness.

If, over and above the Ten Commandments, God shows us the Evangelical Counsels[1] as a more perfect aim for our efforts, he is always careful to accommodate the practice of them to our position and character. As a principal sign of our calling to follow them, he gives us the attraction of grace that makes them easier. He never urges any of us beyond our strength, nor in any way beyond our aptitude. Again, what could be more just?

All you who strive after perfection and who are tempted to discouragement by what you read in the lives of the saints and what you find prescribed in spiritual books, you who are overwhelmed by the terrible ideas of perfection you have formed for yourselves: it is for your consolation that God wills me to write this. Learn what you do not seem to know.

In the realm of nature, the God of all goodness has made easy the things that are universal and necessary—breathing, eating, and sleeping. No less essential in the supernatural realm are love and faithfulness. Therefore the difficulty in achieving them cannot be as great as is generally thought. Consider your own life. Is it not made up of numerous, unimportant little actions? Well, God is quite satisfied with these. They are the very things in which we must cooperate in the work of our perfection. God himself expresses it in terms too clear for us to doubt: "Fear God, and keep his commandments; for that is the whole duty of everyone" (Ecclesiastes 12:13). That is to say, this is all that is required on our part—that is what makes up active faithfulness. If we fulfill our part, God will do the rest.

Grace, working by itself, will achieve marvels that surpass human comprehension. For neither has ear heard nor eye seen, nor has it entered into the mind, what things God plans in his infinite awareness and insight, resolves in his will, and carries out by his power in the soul that is given up entirely to him.

The passive aspect of faithfulness is easier still, since it consists only of accepting what most frequently cannot be avoided, and in bearing with love, consolation, and sweetness what we too often endure with weariness and irritation.

Once more, then, here is the whole sum of holiness. Here is the grain of mustard seed that is the smallest of all the seeds, which, being so tiny, is unrecognized and lost. It is the lost coin of the Gospel, the treasure that we do not search for and do not find, because we imagine it is too far beyond us.

Do not ask how it may be found. It is no secret. The treasure is offered to us at every moment, in every place. Our fellow-creatures, friends, and enemies pour it out liberally for us, and it flows like a fountain through every part of our bodies and souls, even to the very center of our hearts. If we open our mouths wide they will be filled. God's action floods the whole universe; it pervades every creature. Wherever they are, there it is. It goes before them, it goes with them, and it follows them. All we have to do is to allow ourselves to be carried forward on its waves.

Would that it might please God that kings and their ministers, princes of the Church and of the world, priests, soldiers, commoners—in one word, all human beings, might know how easy it is for us to arrive at a sublime holiness! All we have to do is to fulfill the simple duties of a Christian and of our state of life, and bear with submission the crosses involved, and to accept with faith and love the work and suffering that, although we do not search for them, come endlessly to us through God's own providential designs. This is the spirit by which the

Patriarchs and Prophets were moved and made holy before there were so many methods of direction and so many directors of the spiritual life.

This is the spirituality of all ages and conditions. Surely no state of life can be made holy in a more exalted manner or in a more wonderful and easy way than by the simple use of the means that God, the sovereign Director of souls, gives us to do or to suffer at each moment.

CHAPTER 4
Perfection Means Submission to God's Will

The designs of God, the good pleasure of God, the will of God, the action of God, and the gift of his grace are all one and the same thing in the spiritual life. It is God at work in the soul to make it like himself. Perfection is nothing more or less than the faithful cooperation of the soul with this work of God. This work begins, grows, and is completed in our souls secretly and without our knowledge.

Theology is full of theories and explanations of how each soul is brought into this wonderful perfection to the fullest extent of its capacity. We may know all the theories and understand the explanations of this work in the soul, speak and write about them beautifully, or instruct and direct others. But if this knowledge is only head-knowledge, one who possesses it will be like a sick physician compared to simple people who enjoy perfect health, who live and act according to God's designs, and who are guided by God's holy will, even though they are ignorant of theories. When a faithful soul accepts the designs of God and his divine will with simplicity, this holy effect is brought about in it without its knowledge, just as medicine taken obediently will produce health, although the sick person neither knows nor wishes to know anything about medicine. Just as fire warms us, rather than philosophical discussions about fire or knowledge of its effects, so the designs of God and his holy will work in the soul to make it holy—not intellectual speculations concerning the principles or methods that produce holiness in our souls.

When we are thirsty, we must drink; theoretical explanations will not quench our thirst. The desire to know only increases our thirst even more. Therefore, when we thirst after holiness, the desire to know about it only drives it further away. We must put speculation aside and drink in simplicity of all that the will of God sends us, both to do and to suffer. Those things that happen at each moment by God's command or permission are always the holiest, the best, the most divine thing that could happen to us.

CHAPTER 5

The Limited Use of Reading and Other Exercises

All we need to know is how to recognize God's will for the present moment. Any reading we might choose without regard to the will of God is harmful to us. The will of God and obedience to his leading brings us grace, and this grace is what does the work in the depths of our hearts through reading or anything else we do. Without God, books are only vain appearances, deprived of God's life-giving power as far as we are concerned, and they succeed only in emptying the heart by the very satisfaction our reading brings to the mind.

God's will, working in the souls of simple and ignorant persons through suffering or through a few very ordinary actions, produces an abundance of supernatural life in those persons without filling their minds with self-exalting ideas. On the other hand, proud persons who study spiritual books merely out of curiosity, with no concern for the will of God, receive only the dead letter of the law into their minds, and their hearts grow even drier and harder.

God's order of things, God's divine will, are the life of the soul, no matter in what way they work or are obeyed. Whatever may be the relation of God's will to the intelligence, it nourishes the soul and gives growth to it by giving it each moment what is best for it. Nor is one thing more effective than another in producing these happy effects, but rather, whatever God has willed for the present moment. What was best for the moment that has passed is no longer so, because it is no longer the better part: all we have to do is allow it to act and surrender ourselves to it blindly and with perfect trust. It is infinitely wise, powerful, and bountiful to those who trust themselves unreservedly to it, who love and go in search for it alone, and who believe with an unshaken faith and confidence that what it arranges for each moment is best, without searching elsewhere for more or less, and without pausing to consider the connection between these outward circumstances and the will of God. Such consideration would be the seeking of pure self-love.

Nothing is essential, real, or of any value unless it is ordained by God, who adapts all things and makes them suitable to the soul. Aside from God's will, everything is hollow, empty, and vacant: there is nothing but falsehood, vanity, nothingness, shallowness, the letter of the law, death. The will of God is the salvation, health, and life of both body and soul, no matter what may be its ways of reaching us. We must not, then, scrutinize too closely the suitability of things to the mind or the body to form a judgment of their value, because this is of little importance. It is the will of God, given in and through these things, that effectively works to renew the image of Jesus Christ deep within our hearts. We must not attempt to make God's will conform to a law or set limits on it, for it is all-powerful. Whatever ideas the mind may form, whatever feelings the body may experience, even if the mind is tormented with distractions and trouble, or the body with sickness and pain—nevertheless, God's will is always the life of the body and the soul at every moment. In fact, both body and soul, whatever their condition may be, are sustained by God's will alone.

Without it, bread may be poison; with it, poison can be a healthful remedy. Without it, books can only darken the mind; with it, darkness is turned to light. God's will is everything that is good and true in all things. In all things that will unites us to God, and God, infinite in all his perfections, leaves nothing to be desired by the soul that possesses him.

CHAPTER 6

The Limited Use of Intelligence

The mind with all its powers would like to hold first place among all the instruments employed by God, but it must, like a dangerous slave, be reduced to the lowest place. It might be of great service if made use of in a right manner, but it can do much injury if it is not kept in subjection. When the soul longs for outward supports, grace whispers to the heart that God's invisible work is enough. When the soul wishes to forego created means of help at the wrong time, God shows it that such help should be received and used with singleness of heart, in keeping with his established will. We should use such means as tools, not for their own sake, but as though we did not use them, and when we are deprived of them all, we should realize that we lack nothing.

Although God's action is infinite in its power, it can take full possession of our souls only insofar as we are empty of all confidence in our own action. For this confidence, being founded on a false idea of our own ability, excludes God's action. This is the obstacle that is most likely to hinder God's work, for he finds it in the soul itself. As far as outside obstacles are concerned, God can change them at will into powerful aids for our progress. Everything is both equally useful and useless to him. Without his action, everything is as nothing. With it, the tiniest nothing can become everything.

Whatever the value in itself of meditation, contemplation, spoken prayer, interior silence, intuition, quiet retreat, or bustling activity—whatever it may be in itself, even if very desirable—that which God wills at the present moment is best, and everything else must be regarded by the soul as nothing at all.

Thus seeing only God in all things, we must take or leave them all as he pleases, so as to live, to be strengthened, or to hope only by what he ordains, and never by any power or virtue that does not come from him. We ought, at every moment and on all occasions, say with St. Paul, "Lord, what wilt thou have me to do?" (Acts 9:6 KJV), without preferring this or that, but only to accomplish his holy will. "The mind prefers one thing, the body another; but Lord, I desire nothing but to do your holy will. Work, contemplation, or prayer, spoken or silent, active or passive; the prayer of faith or of understanding; universal grace or some specific gift—these are all nothing, Lord, unless your will makes them real and useful. Your holy will alone is the object of my devotion, not any of these *things*, however exalted and sublime they may be, because your grace has been given for the perfection of the heart rather than of the mind."

The presence of God that makes our souls holy is the indwelling of the Holy Trinity in the depths of our hearts when we submit to his holy will. The presence of God resulting from the act of contemplation brings about this intimate union in us in exactly the same way as do other acts that are done according to the will of God. However, it holds first place among them, for it is the most excellent way to unite ourselves to God when he wills us to use it.

There is nothing unlawful, then, in the love and esteem we have for contemplation and other godly exercises, if this love and esteem are directed entirely to the God of all goodness who willingly makes use of these means to unite our souls to himself.

We receive the Prince himself when we receive his personal staff. It would be showing him little respect to neglect his officers under the pretext of wishing to be with him alone.

CHAPTER 7
Attaining Lasting Peace

The soul who is not committed to the will of God alone will find neither its satisfaction nor its sanctification in the various methods—not even in the most excellent devotional exercises. If that which God himself chooses for you does not satisfy you, from whom do you expect to receive what you desire? If you turn from the food prepared for you by God's own will, what food could satisfy a taste so depraved? A soul can be nourished, strengthened, purified, enriched, and made holy only by the fullness of the present moment. What more would you have? Since you can find all that is good here, why search for it anywhere else? Do you know better than God? Since he ordains it this way, why do you want it to be different? Can his wisdom and goodness be deceived? When you find that something is in accord with his divine wisdom and goodness, should you not conclude that it must be the best that could happen? Do you think you will find peace in struggling with the Almighty? Is it not, rather, this resistance, this struggle, too often continued without admitting it even to ourselves, that is the cause of all our inward agitations?

It is only just, therefore, that the soul that is not satisfied with the divine fullness of each present moment should be punished by being unable to find happiness in anything else. If books, the example of the saints, and spiritual conversations take away our soul's peace—if they fill our mind without satisfying it—it is a sign that we have strayed from the path of simple surrender to God's will, and that we are seeking only to please ourselves. The very fullness they offer prevents God from finding an entrance, and we must get rid of these things because they are obstacles to the work of grace. But if God's will ordains that we make use of them, we may receive them just as we do everything else—that is to say, as the means ordained by God, which we accept simply to use as they are, and when their moment has passed, leave them for the duties of the next moment. In fact, there is nothing really good that does not come to us from the order of God, and nothing, however good in itself, can be more effective for making us holy or more capable of giving peace to our souls.

CHAPTER 8
Who Is the Most Holy?

The will of God gives a supernatural and divine value to everything for the soul that is submitted to it. All the duties God's will imposes, all those contained in it, all the matters it touches, become holy and perfect, because the will of God is unlimited in power and makes everything it touches divine.

But in order not to stray either to the right or the left, we should follow such inspirations we believe we have received from God only if we are sure that they will not take us from the duties of our state of life. These duties are the most certain manifestations of God's will, and we should prefer nothing above them. In them there is nothing to fear, nothing to exclude, nothing to be chosen. The moments given to such duties are the most precious and most healthful for our souls because we are sure of accomplishing God's holy will. The entire virtue of what we call holiness lies in faithfulness to what God ordains. Therefore we must refuse nothing and seek after nothing, but accept everything that is ordained from him.

Books and wise counsels, vocal prayer and inward affections, when they are in accord with his will, instruct, guide, and unite us with him. In condemning the use of these means and everything that pertains to the senses, quietism erred greatly, for there are souls that God intends to keep always in this way. Their state of life and their leadings show this clearly enough. It is foolish to picture any kind of self-surrender in which all personal activity is excluded. When God requires action, holiness is to be found in activity.

Besides the duties imposed on everyone by the circumstances of their life, God may require certain actions that are not included in these duties, though not in any way contrary to such duties. A leading and inspiration are then the signs of God's approval. Those who are led by God in this way will find a greater perfection by adding the things that are inspired to those that are commanded, taking the necessary precautions to make sure that these inspirations do not interfere with the duties of our state and the happenstances of Providence. God makes saints as he chooses. They are always made according to his plan and in conformity with his will. This conformity is the truest and most perfect surrender of self.

The duties of one's state of life and what comes from divine Providence are common to all the saints and are what God arranges for everyone in general. The saints live hidden from the world, for the world is so fatal to holiness that they wish to avoid the world's quicksand. But their holiness does not consist in this. Rather, it is in their surrender to the will of God. The more absolute this surrender becomes, the greater their holiness.

We must not look at those whose inner leadings and inspirations are unquestionably valid, and whose virtues are shown in unusual and extraordinary ways, and then conclude that these extraordinary gifts exempt them from self-surrender. As soon as God's will makes duties of these astonishing actions, if they were to refuse to do them simply to fulfill their ordinary duties or the usual inspirations of Providence, they would be resisting God. In that case his holy will would no longer be in charge of the moment, and it would mean they had ceased to practice self-surrender. They must consider their duties in keeping with the designs of God, and follow the path designated by their particular leadings. To carry out their inspirations would then become a duty to which they must be faithful.

And just as there are souls whose whole duty is defined by outward laws, and who should not go beyond it, because God's will has so ordained, so there are others who, in addition to exterior duties, are obliged to be faithful to the inward law imprinted on their hearts. Each of us must follow the path appointed for us. Perfection consists in complete surrender to the will of God, and in fulfilling our normal duties in the most perfect manner possible.

But which state is most perfect? A vain and idle question! To compare the different states as they are in themselves can be of no help to us, since perfection is not found in the amount of work or in the sort of duties given to us. If self-love is the motive of our action, or if it is not immediately crushed when discovered, our supposed abundance of good works will in truth be absolute poverty because it is not coming from God's will.

To give some answer to the question, however, I think that holiness can be measured by the love we have for God, and our desire to please him. The more his will is our guiding principle, and the more we conform to and love his plans, the greater will be our holiness, no matter what means we use. This is what we notice in Jesus, Mary, and Joseph. In their separate lives there is more of love than of greatness, more of the spirit than of matter. It is not written that they searched for holiness of circumstances, but rather holiness in all their circumstances. It must therefore be concluded that one way is not more perfect than another, but that the most perfect way is the one that most closely conforms to God's revealed will, whether it means exterior duties or inward attitudes.

CHAPTER 9
Holiness Made Easy

I believe that if those who are seriously striving after holiness were instructed as to the conduct they ought to follow they would be spared a good deal of trouble. I speak as much of laypersons as of religious. If the former (that is, laypersons) could realize the merit concealed in the actions of each moment of the day—I mean in each of the daily duties and actions belonging to their state of life—and if the latter (that is, those who are members of religious orders) could be persuaded that holiness is found in what seems unimportant to them, they would all indeed be happy. If, in addition, they understood that the crosses sent them by Providence—crosses that they constantly find in the circumstances of their lives—lead them to the highest perfection by a surer and shorter path than extraordinary states or spectacular works, and if they understood that surrender to the will of God is the true philosopher's stone that changes into divine gold all their occupations, troubles, and sufferings, what consolation would be theirs! What courage would they derive from this thought: that in order to acquire the friendship of God and to arrive at eternal glory, they have only to do what they are doing and to suffer what they are already suffering, and that what they waste and count as nothing is enough to bring them the greatest holiness, far more than any extraordinary state or wonderful works!

Dearest God! how much I long to be the missionary of your holy will, to teach everyone that there is nothing so easy, so simple, so within the reach of all, as holiness! I wish that I could make people understand that just as the good and the bad thief had the same things to do and to suffer in order to be holy, so it is with two persons, one of whom is worldly and the other leading an interior and wholly spiritual life. One has no more to do than the other. The one who is made holy gains eternal blessedness by submission to your holy will doing those very things that the other, who is lost, does to please himself, or endures with reluctance and rebellion. The difference is in the heart.

Beloved souls who read this! It will cost you no more than to do what you are doing, to suffer what you are suffering. It is only your heart that must be changed. When I say *heart*, I mean the will. Holiness, then, consists in willing all that God wills for us. Yes! holiness of the heart is a simple "Let it be," a simple conformity of the will with the will of God.

What could be easier, and who can refuse to love a will so kind and good? Let us love God's will, and this love will make everything in us divine.

CHAPTER 10

God's Hand Present Everywhere

All creatures are living in the hand of God. The senses perceive only the physical causes, but faith sees God's hand in all things. Faith believes that Jesus Christ lives in all things, that his divine operation continues to the end of time, and that every passing moment and the tiniest atom contain a portion of this hidden life and mysterious action. The physical creation is a veil concealing the profound mysteries of the divine work. After the Resurrection, Jesus took his disciples by surprise in his various appearances. He showed himself to them under forms that they did not recognize, and, in the very act of making himself known to them, disappeared from their sight. This same Jesus, ever living, ever working, still surprises the soul whose faith is weak and wavering.

There is not a moment in which God is not present with us under the cover of some pain to be endured, some obligation or some duty to be performed, or some consolation to be enjoyed. All that takes place within us, around us, or through us involves and conceals his divine hand.

God's hand is really and truly there, but it is invisibly present, so that we are always surprised and do not recognize his operation until it has ceased. If we could lift the veil, and if we were attentive and watchful, God would continually reveal himself to us, and we would see his hand in everything that happens to us, and rejoice in it. At every event we would exclaim, "It is the Lord!" and we would accept every fresh circumstance as a gift from God. We would consider physical causes as very feeble instruments in the hands of an all-powerful Workman, and we would easily find that we lack nothing, and that God's watchful care disposes him to supply whatever we need at every moment. If only we had faith we would be grateful to all the external means he uses. We would cherish them, and be thankful for them in our hearts, because in the hand of God they have been so useful to us, so favorable to the work of our perfection.

If we lived an uninterrupted life of faith, we would be in uninterrupted fellowship with God and speak to him face to face. Just as the air transmits our words and thoughts, so would all that we are called to do and to suffer transmit the words and thoughts of God to us. All that came to us would be only the embodiment of his word, and in all external events we would see nothing but what is excellent and holy. The glory of God makes this the state of the blessed in heaven, and faith would make it our state on earth. There would be only the difference of means.

Faith is God's interpreter. Without the light of faith, creation speaks to us in vain. It is a writing in coded symbols in which we can find nothing but confusion, a mass of thorns from which no one would expect to hear the voice of God. But faith reveals to us, as it did to Moses, the fire of divine love burning in the midst of the thorn bush. It gives the clue to the coded symbols, and reveals to us in the midst of confusion the wonders of divine wisdom. Faith gives a heavenly face to the whole earth. By faith the heart is raised, is enraptured, and becomes conversant with heavenly things.

Faith is our light in this life. Faith alone grasps the truth without seeing it. By faith we touch what we cannot feel, and see what is invisible to the eye. By faith we view the world as though it did not exist. It is the key to the treasure house, the key to the depths of divine wisdom, the key to the knowledge of God. It is faith that teaches us the emptiness, the falseness of created things. By it God reveals and manifests himself in all things. It is faith that tears the veil aside to reveal the eternal reality.

All that we see is nothing but vanity and falsehood. Reality can be found only in God. How far above our illusions are the ways of God! How is it that although continually warned that everything that happens in the world is only a shadow, a figure, a mystery of faith, we are guided by human feelings and judge events by the natural sense of things, which after all is only an enigma?

We fall into this trap like fools, instead of raising our eyes to the principle, the source, the origin of things. There, they all have other names and other qualities. There, everything is supernatural, divine, and sanctifying. There, everything is part of the completeness of Jesus Christ, and each circumstance is as a stone toward the building of the heavenly Jerusalem, and everything helps to build a dwelling for us in that marvelous city.

We live according to what we see and feel, and wander like mad persons in a labyrinth of darkness and illusion for lack of the light of faith that would guide us safely through it. By means of faith we would be able to aspire after God and live for him alone, unheeding and rising above mere figures of the senses.

CHAPTER 11
Recognizing God's Hand by Faith

Those who are enlightened by faith judge things in a very different way from those who have only their senses to guide them and ignore the inestimable treasures they conceal. One who knows the king in disguise treats him very differently from another who, judging by appearances alone, fails to recognize his royalty and treats him as a commoner. In the same way the soul that recognizes the will of God in even the smallest circumstances, even in those that are most distressing and fatal, receives them all with equal joy, pleasure, and respect. That soul throws open all its doors to receive with honor what others fear and fly from in horror. The outward appearance may be humble and contemptible, but beneath this abject garb, the heart discovers and honors the majesty of the King. The more this majesty abases itself to visit the soul in this secret and modest way, the more love for him fills the heart.

I cannot describe what the heart feels when it accepts the divine will in such humble, poor, and lowly disguises. How the sight of God, poor and humble and lodged in a stable, lying on straw, weeping and trembling, pierced the loving heart of Mary! Ask the inhabitants of Bethlehem what they thought of the Child. You know what answer they gave, and how they would have paid court to him if he had been lodged in a palace surrounded by the honor due to princes.

Then ask Mary, Joseph, the Magi, and the Shepherds. They will tell you that they found in this extreme poverty an unexplainable something that made God greater and more loveable. Faith is strengthened, increased, and enriched by those very things that escape the senses: the less there is to see, the more there is to believe. To adore Jesus on the Mount of Transfiguration, to love the will of God in extraordinary things, does not show as much faith as loving the will of God in ordinary things and adoring Jesus on the cross. For faith cannot be said to be real, living faith, until it is tested and has triumphed over everything that would destroy it. This war with the senses enables faith to win a more glorious victory. To consider God equally good in the most petty and ordinary events as in great and unusual ones is to have a faith that is not ordinary, but is itself great and extraordinary.

To be satisfied with the present moment is to delight in and to adore God's will in all that comes to us to do or suffer through the succession of events each passing moment brings. Those who have this disposition adore God with redoubled love and respect, even in the greatest humiliation. Nothing hides him from the piercing eye of faith. The louder the senses exclaim, "This cannot be from God!" the closer they press this bundle of myrrh from the hand of the Bridegroom. Nothing daunts them; nothing repels them.

Mary remained steadfast at the foot of the cross when the disciples fled. She recognized her Son in that Face that was spat upon and bruised, covered with mud and spit. The wounds that disfigured him only made him more loveable and adorable in the eyes of this tender Mother. The more awful were the blasphemies uttered against him, so much the deeper became her veneration.

In the same way, the life of faith is nothing less than the continued pursuit of God through all that disguises, disfigures, destroys, and, so to speak, annihilates him. It is in very truth a reproduction of the life of Mary, who, from the Stable to Calvary, remained unalterably united to that God whom the world despised, persecuted, and abandoned. Just so, faithful souls, despite a constant succession of trials, veils of darkness, and illusive appearances that make his will difficult to recognize, persistently follow him and love him even to death on the cross.

They know that, heedless of all disguises, they must run after the light of this divine Sun. From its rising to its setting, however dark or thick the clouds may be that hide it, this Sun enlightens, warms, and inflames the faithful hearts that bless, praise, and contemplate him at every point of his mysterious journey across their sky.

Hurry, then, happy, faithful, untiring souls, to this beloved Spouse, who with giant strides passes from one end of the heavens to the other! Nothing will be able to hide him from you. He moves above the smallest blade of grass as above the mighty cedar. The grains of sand are under his feet no less than the huge mountains. Wherever your foot may rest, he has passed, and you have only to follow him faithfully to find him wherever you may go.

What a delightful peace we enjoy when we have learned by faith to find God through all his creatures as through a transparent veil. Then darkness becomes light, and bitterness becomes sweet. Faith, showing us things as they are, transforms their ugliness into beauty and their malice into goodness. Faith is the mother of gentleness, confidence, and joy. It cannot help feeling tenderness and compassion for its enemies, by whose means it is so immeasurably enriched. The more malignant the action of the creature, the more profitable God makes it to the soul. While the human instrument seeks to injure us, the divine Workman does his work, making use of its very malice to remove from the soul all that is injurious to it.

The will of God has nothing but sweetness, grace, and treasures for the surrendered soul. It is impossible to place too much confidence in it, or to surrender oneself to it too utterly.

It always acts for and desires that which contributes most to our perfection, provided we allow it to act. Faith does not doubt. The more unfaithful, uncertain, and rebellious are the senses, the louder faith cries, "All is well! It is the will of God!" There is nothing that the eye of faith does not penetrate, nothing that the power of faith does not overcome. It passes through the thick darkness, and, no matter what clouds may gather, it goes straight to the truth, grasps it in firm embrace, and never lets it go.

CHAPTER 12

Finding the Will of God

If we are able to greet each passing moment as the manifestation of the will of God, we will find in it all our heart can desire. What could there be more reasonable, more perfect, more divine than the will of God? Could any change of time or place or circumstance alter or increase its infinite value? If you possess the secret of discovering it at every moment and in everything, then you possess all that is most precious and worthy to be desired. What is it that you are searching for, you who desire to become holy? Give full scope to your longings. Your wishes need have no measure, no limit. However much you may desire, I can show you how to attain it, even though it may be infinite. There is never a moment in which I cannot enable you to obtain all that you can desire.

The present moment is always filled with infinite treasure. It contains more than you have the capacity to hold. Faith is the measure of these treasures: according to your faith you will receive. Love also is the measure. The more the heart loves, the more it desires, and the more it desires, the more it will receive. The will of God is constantly before you like an immense, inexhaustible ocean that no human heart can fathom; but none of us can receive from it more than we have the capacity to contain. It is necessary to enlarge this capacity by faith, confidence, and love.

The whole universe cannot fill the human heart, for its capacity is greater than anything other than God. It is on a higher plane than the material creation, and for this reason nothing material can satisfy it. The divine will is a deep sea, the surface of which is the present moment. If you plunge into this sea you will find it infinitely vaster than your desires. Offer no homage to creatures; do not adore your own illusions. They can neither give you anything nor deprive you of anything. Receive your fullness from the will of God alone, and it will not leave you empty. Adore it, put it first, before all things. Tear all disguises from vain pretenses and forsake them all, going straight to the sole reality.

The reign of faith is death to the senses; it injures them beyond reclaim and destroys them. The senses worship the physical. Faith adores God's divine will. Destroy the idols of the senses and they will weep and rebel, but faith must triumph, because the will of God cannot be separated from it. When the senses are terrified, famished, despoiled, or crushed, then it is that faith is enriched and nourished. Faith laughs at these calamities as the commander of an impregnable fortress mocks at the useless attacks of an impotent foe.

When we recognize the will of God and surrender entirely to it, then God gives himself to us and we experience the most powerful assistance in all difficulties. Thus we enjoy great happiness in this coming of God, and the more we learn to surrender ourselves to his all-adorable will at every moment, the more joy we have.

God Revealed in Ordinary Circumstances

The written word of God is full of mystery. His word expressed in the events of the world is no less so. These are two sealed books, and of both it can be said, "the letter kills."

God is the center of faith. All that emanates from this center is hidden in the deepest mystery. This word and these events are, so to speak, feeble rays from a sun obscured by clouds. It is vain to expect to see with our mortal eyes the rays of this sun. Even the eyes of our soul are blind to God and his works. Obscurity here reigns rather than clear light; knowledge itself is ignorance, and we see without seeing. The Holy Scripture is the mysterious Word of an even more mysterious God. And the events of the world are the obscure language of this same hidden God who is not readily investigated, interpreted, or understood. They are mere drops of the ocean, but an ocean of shadows. Every drop of the stream, every brook of water partakes of the nature of their source.

The fall of the angels, the fall of humanity, the impiety and idolatry of humankind before and after the Flood up to the time of the Patriarchs, who knew and told their children the history of Creation and of its still-recent preservation from the universal Flood—these are indeed very obscure words of Holy Scripture! It seems incredible that when the Messiah came, only a handful of persons should be preserved from idolatry in the general ruin and overthrow of faith throughout the world. It seems unbelievable that evil is always dominant, always powerful. It seems incredible that the little band of those who uphold the truth should always be persecuted and ill-treated. Consider the treatment of Jesus Christ. Think of the plagues of the Book of Revelation—yet these are the words of God. They are what God revealed. It is what God has dictated. And the effect of these terrible mysteries, which endure till the end of time, are still the living word, teaching us God's wisdom, God's power, God's goodness. All the events in the history of the world show forth these divine attributes and preach the same Word, who is worthy of our worship. We must believe it, for—and what a pity this is!—we cannot see it.

What is God saying by the existence of infidels, heretics, and all the other enemies of the Church? Surely they point to the infinite perfections of God. Pharaoh and all the evil persons who followed him are allowed to exist only for that purpose, though truly, unless we look at them with the eye of faith, the end of all these would seem most contrary to the divine glory. We must close our eyes to what is external and cease to reason in order to see the divine mysteries.

You speak, Lord, to humankind in general in great public events. All revolutions are only the waves of the sea of your Providence, waves that stir up storms and tempests in the minds of those who question your mysterious actions. You speak, also, to each individual soul by the circumstances occurring at every moment. But instead of receiving what is obscure and mysterious in these your words, and hearing your voice in all the occurrences of life, they see only the outward aspect, or they see chance, or the caprice of others, and they find fault in everything. They would like to add to, diminish, reform—in fact, they allow themselves absolute liberty with these living words of God, while they would consider it a sacrilege to alter a comma of the Holy Scriptures. The Scriptures they revere: "They are the Word of God," they tell you. "They are true and holy. If we cannot understand them, that makes them all the more wonderful and we must give glory to God for the depth of his wisdom."

All this is perfectly true, dear souls, but when you read God's word from moment to moment, not written with ink on paper, but on your soul with suffering and all the daily actions you have to perform, do these words not deserve some attention on your part? How is it that you cannot see the will of God in all this? Instead, you find fault with everything that happens, and nothing pleases you. Do you not see that you are measuring everything by the senses and by reason, not by faith, the only true standard?

And since you read the Word of God in the Holy Scriptures with the eye of faith, you are gravely mistaken when you read this same word in God's other operations with any other eyes.

CHAPTER 14
God's Word Written on the Heart

"Jesus Christ is the same yesterday and today and forever," says the Apostle (Hebrews 13:8). From the beginning of the world he was, as God, the source of the life of righteous souls. From the first moment of his incarnation, his humanity shared this prerogative of his divinity. He is working within us throughout our whole lives. The time that will elapse till the end of the world is only as a day, and this day abounds with his action. Jesus Christ lived and lives still. He began in himself and he continues in his saints a life that will never end.

Life of Jesus! including and extending beyond all the ages of time! life working new wonders of grace at every moment! If no one is capable of understanding all that could be written of the earthly life of Jesus, all that he did and said while he was on earth—if the Gospel merely outlines a few of its features—how many Gospels would have to be written to record the history of all the moments of this mystical life of Jesus Christ that multiplies miracles to infinity and eternity! If the beginning of his natural life is so hidden and yet so fruitful, what can be said of the effect of that life of which every age of the world is the history?

The Holy Spirit has pointed out some moments in that ocean of time in the infallible words of the Holy Scriptures. In them we see the hidden and mysterious ways by which he has manifested Jesus Christ to the world. Amid the confusion of the races of humankind, we can follow the channels and veins that distinguish the origin, race, and genealogy of the Firstborn. The entire Old Testament is only an outline of the profound mystery of this divine work; it contains only what is necessary to reach the coming of Jesus Christ. The Holy Spirit kept all the rest hidden among the treasures of his wisdom. From this vast sea of divine action, only a tiny stream appears, and when this has reached Jesus, it is lost again in the Apostles and swallowed up in the Book of Revelation. So the history of this divine action, consisting of the life of Jesus in the souls of the righteous to the very end of time, can only be perceived by faith alone.

As the truth of God has been made known by word, the love of God is made known by deeds. The Holy Spirit continues to carry on the work of our Savior. While helping the Church to preach the gospel of Christ, he himself is writing his own gospel in the hearts of the faithful. All their actions, all the moments of their lives, make up the gospel of the Holy Spirit. The souls of the saints are the paper, their sufferings and actions are the ink. The Holy Spirit, by the pen of his actions, writes a living gospel, but we can read it only when it has been taken out of the press of this life and published on the day of eternity.

Wonderful story! What a glorious book the Holy Spirit is now writing! It is still on the press. There is never a day when the type is not being set, ink applied, and sheets printed. But we are still in the night of faith. The paper is blacker than the ink, and there is great confusion in the type. It is written in letters that belong to another world, and there is no understanding of it but in heaven itself.

If we could perceive this life of God, and see all creatures, not as they are in themselves, but as instruments of his will, and if again, we could perceive his life in all his creatures and understand how his action animates and impels them all to press forward in different ways, mingling them, assembling them, scattering them, yet pushing them all to the same point by different means, we would recognize that everything in this divine work has its reason, its measure, its connection with God's overall work. But how can we read this book whose letters are foreign to us, whose type is reversed, and whose pages are blotted with ink?

If the blending of the twenty-six letters of our alphabet results in such incomprehensible diversity that they can be used to write an almost infinite number of different volumes, all admirable, who can explain what God is doing in the universe? Who can read and understand the meaning of so vast a book in which every single letter has its own particular significance and contains in its littleness the most profound mysteries? Mysteries can be neither seen nor felt. They are objects of faith. Faith alone judges their worth and truth only by their source, because they are so obscure in themselves that all their external appearances serve only to conceal them and mislead those who judge by reason alone.

Teach me, Divine Spirit, to read in this book of life. I desire to become your disciple and, like a little child, to believe what I cannot understand and cannot see. It is enough for me that it is my Lord who speaks. He says this! he pronounces that! he arranges the letters in such a fashion! he makes himself heard in such a manner! That is enough. I judge that all is exactly as he says. I do not see the reason, but he is the infallible truth; therefore all that he says, all that he does is true. He groups his letters to form a word, and different letters again to form another word. The word may have three letters, or it may have six. Then no more are necessary, and fewer would be nonsense. He alone who knows all the thoughts of mortals can bring these letters together to express it. Everything has significance, everything has a perfect meaning. This line purposely ends here. Not a comma is missing, nor is there one useless period. I believe that now, but in the glory to come, when so many mysteries will be revealed, I shall see plainly what I understand so dimly.

Then what appears so complicated, so perplexing, so foolish, so inconsistent, so imaginary, will charm and delight me eternally with the beauty, order, knowledge, wisdom, and inconceivable wonders I shall find in it.

CHAPTER 15
Christians' Disregard of God's Action

What unfaithfulness there is in the world! How unworthy are human thoughts of God! We constantly complain of God's action in a way we would not use toward the lowest of workmen about his trade. We would reduce God's action to the limits and rules of our feeble reason. We presume to imagine that we can improve on his acts. These are nothing but complaints and murmurings.

We are surprised at the treatment endured by Jesus at the hands of the Jews. Divine love! adorable Will of God! infallible truth! in what way are you treated? Can God's will ever occur at other than the proper time? Can it be mistaken? "But there is this business of mine! I require such and such a thing! The necessary helps for my purpose have been taken from me. That person thwarts all my good works. Is it not most unreasonable? This illness comes on just when my health is most important to me." To all this there is only one answer: that the will of God is the only thing necessary; therefore, what it does not grant must be useless.

My good souls, nothing is lacking to you. If you only knew what these events really are that you call misfortunes, accidents, and disappointments, and in which you can see nothing but what you consider out of place or unreasonable, you would be deeply ashamed. You would blame yourselves for your complaints as blasphemous. But you never think of these happenings as being the will of God, and his adorable will is blasphemed by his own dear children who refuse to acknowledge it.

When you were on earth, my dear Jesus, you were treated as a demoniac. They called you a Samaritan. And now, although it is acknowledged that you live and work through all the centuries of time, how is your adorable will received—that will that is worthy of all blessing and praise? Has one moment passed from the creation of the world to the present time, and will there pass one from now to the day of judgment in which the holy name of God is not worthy of praise—that name that fills all the ages and everything that happens in them, and makes them holy? What? Can the will of God do me harm? Shall I be afraid, or run away from the will of God? And where shall I look to find anything better if I dread God's purpose for me, his will in my regard?

We ought to listen attentively to that inner voice in the depths of our hearts every moment. If our understanding and reason do not understand or grasp the truth and goodness of these words, is it not because they are incapable of appreciating divine truths? Should we be amazed that our reason is confused by mysteries? When God speaks it is a mystery, and therefore a deathblow to my senses and my reason, for it is the nature of mysteries to confound both. Mystery makes the soul live by faith; everything else sees it as nothing but a contradiction. God's action by one and the same stroke kills and gives life: the more we feel the death to the senses and reason, the more convinced should we become that it is bringing life to the soul. The darker the mystery, the more light it contains. This is why a simple soul finds nothing more divine than that which has the least appearance of being divine. The life of faith is a continual struggle against the senses.

CHAPTER 16

The Hidden Work of Divine Love

What great truths are hidden from the eyes even of Christians who think that they are the most enlightened! How few among them understand that every cross, every circumstance, every leading of the will of God, gives us God himself in a way that can best be explained by comparing them with the most majestic mystery of all, the Holy Eucharist.

Yet what is more certain? Does not reason as well as faith reveal to us the presence of divine love in all creatures, and in all the events of life, just as indisputably as the words of Jesus Christ and of the Church reveal the presence of the sacred flesh of our

Savior under the Eucharistic elements? Do we not know that by all created things, and by every event, God's love desires to unite itself to us? Do we not know that he has ordained, arranged, or permitted everything that concerns us and everything that happens to us, with a view to this union? This is the sole end of all his designs. To attain this he uses the worst as well as the best of his creatures, and the most distressing events as well as those that are pleasant and agreeable. And the more naturally repellant the means of that union, the more deserving of esteem it becomes.

If this is true, why should not each moment of our lives become a form of communion with the love of God? And why should not this communion of every moment produce as much fruit in our souls as that which we receive in the Communion of the Body and Blood of the Son of God? The holy Eucharist, it is true, has a sacramental efficacy that the "sacrament of the present moment" cannot have, but on the other hand, how much more frequently can this form of communion be repeated! And how greatly may its value be increased by the growing perfection of our dispositions toward it! Consequently, how true it is that the more holy the life, the more mysterious it becomes by its apparent simplicity and lowliness!

Heavenly banquet! Never-ending feast! God ever given and received in utter infirmity, weakness, and nothingness! That which human nature abhors and human reason rejects, God chooses and makes into mysteries, sacraments of love, and by that which seems as if it would do most harm to souls, he gives himself to them as often and as much as they desire to possess him.

CHAPTER 17
Especially For Us

We can be truly instructed only by the words that God speaks to us personally. No one grows in knowledge of God either by reading books or by curious historical research. These means give us only a vain and empty knowledge, which serves only to confuse us and inflate us with pride.

That which truly instructs us is what comes to us by the will of God from moment to moment. This is the knowledge gained through experience, which Christ himself was pleased to acquire before teaching others. In fact, this was the only knowledge in which he could grow, according to the expression of the holy Gospel (Luke 2:52). This is because, being God, there was no degree of speculative knowledge that he did not already possess. Therefore if this experimental knowledge was useful to the Incarnate Word himself, it is absolutely necessary for us if we would touch the hearts of those whom God sends to us.

We know perfectly only what we have learned by experience through suffering or action. This is the school of the Holy Spirit, who speaks the words of life to the heart, and all that we say to others should come from this source. Whatever we read, whatever we see, becomes divine knowledge only by the fruitfulness, the virtue, the light that this experience gives. Without this experiential knowledge, all our learning is like dough made without yeast, lacking the salt and seasoning of experience. Without this experiential knowledge, we have only vague, untried ideas to act on. We are like the dreamer who, though he knows all the highways of the world, misses the road to his own house.

Therefore we have only to listen to God from moment to moment in order to become learned in the knowledge by which the saints lived, which is all practice and experience.

Set aside what is said to others, but listen to what is said to you and for you. You will find enough in that to exercise your faith, because this interior language of God, by its very obscurity, exercises, purifies, and increases your faith.

CHAPTER 18
The Ever-Flowing Spring of Holiness

All you who thirst, learn that you have not far to go to find the spring of living waters! It springs forth quite close to you in the present moment. Therefore hurry to approach it. Why, with the spring so near, do you tire yourselves running after shallow brooks that only tease your thirst? They measure stingily the water they give us, while only the spring itself is inexhaustible. If you wish to think, write, and talk like apostles, prophets, and saints, abandon yourselves as they did to God's inspiration.

Love unknown! We think that your wonders are past and finished, and that all we can do is copy the ancient volumes and quote your words out of the past! And we do not see that your unceasing action is an infinite source of new thoughts, new sufferings, new works, new patriarchs, new prophets, new apostles, new saints, who have no need to copy each other's lives or writings, but only to live in perpetual self-surrender to our secret operations.

We like to speak of "the first ages of the Church—the times of the saints." Are not all times the effect of God's action, the working of his divine will, including all moments, filling them, making them holy, and making them supernatural? Has there ever been a method of self-surrender to God's will that is not still practicable? Did the saints from the earliest ages have any other secret of holiness than that of becoming what God's will was seeking to make them from moment to moment? And will this operation not continue even to the end of time to pour out its grace on those who give themselves unreservedly to it?

Yes, dear eternal Love! Love eternally fruitful and full of wonder! Yes, Will of God! You are my book, my doctrine, my knowledge. In you are my thoughts, my words, my deeds, my crosses. It is not by consulting your other works that I can become what you would make me, but only by accepting you in all things, in that one royal way, that ancient way, the way of our ancestors, the way of self-surrender to your will. I will think like them, speak like them, be enlightened as they were. In this way, I will imitate them, quote them, and copy them in everything.

CHAPTER 19
The Present Moment Manifests
the Coming of God's Kingdom

The present moment is like an ambassador who declares the will of God. The heart must ever answer, "Let it be so." Then the soul will go steadily on by all means toward its target and goal—never pausing in its course, spreading its sails to all winds. All routes and methods advance it equally in its journey toward the great sea, the infinite. Everything becomes an instrument of making us holy. The soul always finds the "one thing needed" in the present moment.

It is no longer a matter of either prayer or silence, privacy or conversation with others, reading or writing, thinking or abandonment of thought, searching for spirituality or avoiding excessive concern with it, abundance or lack, illness or health, life or death; the one thing needed is simply what comes to the soul each moment by the will of God. This includes the stripping, the self-denial, the renunciation of earthly things, in order that the soul may be nothing in itself or live for itself, but may live wholly by God's will, and at his good pleasure content itself with the duty of the present moment, as though that were the one thing in the whole world.

If whatever comes to such a surrendered soul is "the one thing needed," we see clearly that we can lack nothing and should never complain. If we grumble, we lack faith and are living by reason and the senses, which, failing to recognize the sufficiency of grace, are always discontented.

To hallow the name of God is, in the language of Scripture, to love him, to adore him, and to recognize his holiness in all things. Things, like words, do indeed proceed from the mouth of God. The events of each moment are divine thoughts expressed by created objects. Thus, all those things by which he makes his will known to us are so many names, so many words by which he shows us his will. In itself this will is one, singular. It bears only one unknown, inexpressible name, but it is multiplied infinitely in its effects and takes on their names. To hallow the name of God is to know, adore, and love the Inexpressible One who is expressed by this name. It is also to know, adore, and love his blessed will at all times, in all its effects, seeing all things as so many veils, shadows, and names of this eternally holy will. It is holy in all its works, holy in all its words, holy in all its forms of manifestation, holy in all the names it bears.

It was in this way that Job hallowed the name of God. That holy man blessed his terrible desolation that expressed the will of God. He called it not *ruin*, but one of God's names, and blessing it he declared that this divine will, expressed by the most terrible afflictions, was ever holy, no matter what name or form it might bear.

David also hallowed the name of God at all times and in all places. Therefore it is by this continual discovery, by this manifestation, this revelation of the will of God in all things that God's kingdom reigns within us, that God's will is done on earth as it is in heaven, that God gives us our daily bread.

Surrender to God's will contains the essence of that incomparable prayer that Christ himself has taught us. We repeat it vocally several times a day according to the teaching of God and his holy Church, but we utter it in the depth of our hearts each moment that we lovingly receive or suffer whatever is ordained by his sacred will. What the lips need words and time to express, the heart effectively utters with each beat. In this way simple souls are called to bless God in the depth of their hearts. They sigh over their inability to praise him as they would like, yet God gives these souls his grace and favor by the very means that seem to deprive them of these blessings. This is the secret of God's wisdom, to impoverish the senses while it enriches the heart, and to fill the heart in proportion to the aching void the senses experience.

Let us learn then to recognize the imprint of the will of God, of his worthy name in the event of each moment.

How holy is that name! It is only right therefore to bless and receive it as a form of sacrament that by its own power makes holy the souls in which it finds no obstacle to its action. Can we do anything other than to infinitely value whatever bears this majestic name? It is divine manna that falls from heaven in order to strengthen us continually in grace. It is a kingdom of holiness that comes into the soul. It is the bread of angels that is given on earth as it is in heaven. No moment can be unimportant, since all moments contain treasures of grace and the food of angels.

Yes, Lord, let your kingdom come into my heart to make it holy, to nourish it, to purify it, to render it victorious over all my enemies. How insignificant is this precious moment in the eyes of the world, yet how great to the eye that is enlightened by faith! And can I call little that which is great in the eye of my Father who reigns in heaven? All that comes from there is most excellent. All that descends from there bears the imprint of its origin.

CHAPTER 20
God's Will Brings Us to Holiness

It is only because they do not know how to make use of God's action that so many Christians spend their lives anxiously pursuing a multitude of methods of perfection. These might prove useful if ordained by God's will, but they actually become injurious the moment they keep us from simply surrendering ourselves to God's will. These multiplied means cannot give what we will find only in the will of God—the principle of all life that is constantly with us, and that stamps each of its instruments with its own character and causes its original and unique action in us.

Jesus has given us a teacher to whom we do not pay sufficient attention. He speaks to every heart, and to each one he utters the word of life, the only word applicable to us. But we do not hear it. We want to know what he has said to others and do not listen to what is said to us. We do not sufficiently regard circumstances as having been given a supernatural significance by God's action. We should always accept them with the perfect confidence they merit, with an open heart and with generosity, sure that nothing will harm those who receive them this way. This limitless activity, which is the same from the beginning to the end of time, goes on every moment, giving itself in all its greatness and strength to the simple soul who adores it, loves it, and rejoices in it alone.

You would be delighted, you say, to find an opportunity of dying for God's sake. Such heroism enchants you. To lose all, to die, forsaken and alone, to sacrifice your life for others—such are the glorious deeds that charm you!

As for me, Lord, let me glorify your will in all things. In it, I find all the happiness of martyrdom, bodily austerities, and the sacrifice of self for others. Your will is enough, and I am content to live and to die as it decrees. It pleases me more for its own sake than all the means it uses and the effects it produces, because it permeates all things and makes them divine, and transforms them all into itself. It is heaven on earth to me, and all my moments are full of God's action. So, living or dying, I shall always remain content with that.

Yes, my Beloved, I shall no longer single out times or ways, but shall welcome you always and in any fashion. It seems to me, divine Will, as if you had revealed your immensity to me. I will walk from now on in the bosom of your infinity, you who are the same today, yesterday, and forever. Streams of unceasing mercy have their springs in you. From you they begin and continue, and they are changed at your will. No longer will I search for you within the narrow limits of a book or the life of a saint, or of some sublime idea. No, these are only drops of that great ocean that covers every created thing. Your divine will floods them all. They are only atoms that disappear in this unfathomable sea. I will no longer look for your will merely in the thoughts of spiritual persons. No longer will I beg my bread from door to door. I will depend on no creature, but I will live as the child of an infinitely good, wise, and powerful Father whom I desire to please and make happy. I would live as I believe, and since your activity works in everything and at every moment to make me holy, I will draw my life from this great and boundless reservoir, ever present and ever available in the most practical way.

Is there any creature anywhere whose action equals that of God? And since this uncreated Hand directs all that comes to me, shall I go in search of aid from created things? Such creatures are powerless, ignorant, and indifferent to me, and I should die of thirst rushing from one fountain to another, from one stream to another, when there is a sea at hand whose waters surround me on every side.

Yes, all that happens to me becomes bread to nourish me, soap to cleanse me, fire to purify me, a chisel to carve heavenly features on me. Everything is a channel of grace for my needs. The very thing I searched for everywhere else searches incessantly for me, and gives itself to me by means of all created things.

Love of God, will we never see that you meet us at every step, while we search for you here and there, where you are not to be found? How foolish to be in open country and not breathe its pure air! to search for a spot on which to place my foot when the path is smooth before me; to thirst when there is a whole flood of water at my service; to hunger for God when I may find him and taste him and find his will present in everything!

Good people, do you search for the secret of belonging to God? The only way is to make use of everything God sends you. Everything leads to this union. Everything may perfect it except sin and that which is contrary to your duty. You have only to accept all that God sends and let it do its work in you.

Everything is intended to guide, uphold, and support you. Everything is the hand of God. God's action is vaster and more present to you than the elements of earth, air, and water. God will even enter by means of all the senses, provided you use them only as he ordains, because you must guard them and close them to all that is contrary to his will. There is not a single atom in your frame, even the marrow of your bones, that is not formed by divine power. From that power everything proceeds. By it all things are made. Your very life-blood flows through your veins by movement his power imparts. All the variations of your system, between strength and weakness, sluggishness and liveliness, life and death, are divine means put in motion to bring you to holiness. Under his will, every bodily state becomes an operation of grace. All your thoughts, all your emotions, whatever their apparent source, proceed from this invisible hand. No created mind or heart can teach you what his divine action will do in you. You will learn it through experience. Your life flows on unceasingly into this unfathomable Sea, where we have only to love and accept as best what each present moment brings, with perfect trust in God's divine action, his will that can only work for good.

Yes, divine Love! All souls might attain supernatural, praiseworthy, incomparably sublime states if they would only be satisfied with your will in action!

Yes, if they would just leave matters in this divine hand, they would attain a notable degree of holiness! Everyone would arrive at it because it is offered to all. You have only to open your heart and God will act. Every soul possesses in you, God, an infinitely perfect model, and by your action you work ceaselessly to make us in your image. If we were faithful, we would all live, act, and speak divinely. We would not need to copy one another, but would be shaped individually through the most ordinary things.

How, dearest God, can I make your children appreciate what is offered to them? Must I, possessing a treasure that could make the whole world rich, see beloved souls perish in poverty? Must I watch them withering like plants in a desert when I can show them the source of living waters?

Come, simple souls, you who have no feeling of devotion, no talent, not even the first elements of instruction—you who cannot understand a single spiritual term, who stand astonished at the eloquence of the learned whom you admire. Come, and I will teach you a secret that will place you far beyond these clever minds. I will make perfection so easy you will find it everywhere and in everything. I will unite you to God, and he will hold you by the hand from the moment you begin to practice what I tell you. Come, not to learn the map of this spiritual country, but to possess it, to walk in it at your ease without fear of losing your way. Come, not to study the theory of God's grace, or to learn what it has done in the past and is still doing, but simply to be open yourself to what it can do. You do not need to know what it has said to others, or repeat words intended only for them, words that you have overheard. His grace will speak to you, yourself, what is best for you.

CHAPTER 21
Modeled After the Incarnate Word

The workings of God within us carry out in the course of time the designs that Eternal Wisdom has formed in regard to everything. In God all things have their own design, and his wisdom alone knows what that is. Though you read the will of God in regard to others, this knowledge cannot direct you in anything. In the Incarnate Word, in God himself, is the design after which you were meant to be formed and that is the model of his work in you. In the Word, the divine action sees that to which every soul must be conformed. The Holy Scriptures contain one part of this design, and the divine activity formed by the Holy Spirit within the soul completes the design set forth by the Word. We must understand that the only way of receiving the impression of this eternal design is to remain quietly submissive to it, and that neither effort nor mental speculation can help us to attain it.

Is it not evident that a work such as this cannot be accomplished by subtlety of mind, skill, or intelligence, but can only follow on our submissive self-surrender to God's will, yielding ourselves like metal to a mold, or canvas to the brush, or stone in the hands of the sculptor? Is it not clear that knowledge of all the divine mysteries that the will of God carries out in all ages is not what makes us conformable to the design the Word has conceived for us? No, it is the distinctive mark of the divine Hand. This imprint is not engraved on our minds by ideas, but in the will by its submission to the will of God.

The wisdom of the simple soul consists in being content with its own business, in confining itself within the boundary of its path, and not going beyond its limits. It is not curious about God's ways of acting, but is content with God's will in regard to itself, making no effort to discover hidden meanings by comparisons or conjectures, but only desiring to understand what each moment reveals. It listens to the voice of the Word when it sounds in the depths of the heart. It does not ask what the divine Bridegroom has said to others, but is satisfied with what it receives for itself, so that moment by moment, by everything, however insignificant or whatever its nature, the soul is made holy without knowing it. In this way the Bridegroom speaks to his Bride, by the solid effects of his actions, which the soul accepts with loving gratitude and without curious examination.

Thus the spirituality of such a soul is perfectly simple, absolutely solid, permeating its whole being. Its actions are not determined by ideas or by a tumult of words, which by themselves would serve only to inflate pride. People make great use of the intellect in piety, yet it is of little use, and often detrimental to true piety. We must make use only of what God's will gives us to do or to suffer. We must not forsake this divine essential to occupy our minds with the historic wonders of God's work, but rather we should increase these wonders by our own faithfulness.

The marvels of these works of God, which we read about to satisfy our curiosity, often tend only to disgust us with things that seem trifling, but by which, if we do not despise them, God's love accomplishes very great things in us. Foolish creatures that we are! We admire, we bless God's action in written history, but when his love is ready to continue this writing on our hearts, we keep moving the paper and prevent its writing by our curiosity, to see what it is doing in us and what it is accomplishing elsewhere.

Divine Love, forgive these defects. I can see them all in myself, and I have not yet learned what it is to abandon myself to your hand. I have not yet yielded myself to the mold. I have walked through all your workshops and admired all your works of art, but have not as yet had the self-surrender needed to receive even the bare outlines of your brush. But at last I have found you, my dear Master, Teacher, Father, my beloved Friend.

Now I will be your disciple. I will attend no other school than yours. I return, like the prodigal, hungering for your bread. I relinquish the ideas that tend only to satisfy my curiosity. I will no longer run after teachers and books. No, I will use them only as your holy will ordains them, not for my gratification but to obey you, by accepting all that you send me. I will confine myself solely to the duty of the present moment in order to prove my love and leave you free to do with me what you will.

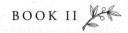

BOOK II

THE STATE OF BEING SURRENDERED TO GOD'S WILL

When the Soul Lives in God

There is a time when the soul lives in God and a time when God lives in the soul. What is appropriate to one of these times is not fitting to the other.

When God lives in the soul, it should surrender itself completely to his providence. When the soul lives in God, it must take trouble to obtain for itself regularly and carefully every possible means to achieve union with him. The whole procedure is marked out—the readings, the examinations of conscience, the resolutions. Its guide is always present; everything is by rule, even the hours for conversation.

When God lives in the soul, it has nothing left of self, but only that which the Spirit imparts to it moment by moment. Nothing is provided for the future, no road is mapped out, but the soul is like a child who can be led wherever one pleases, and has nothing but feeling to distinguish between what is offered to it. No more books with marked passages for these souls; often they are even deprived of a regular spiritual director, for God allows them no other support than himself. They dwell in darkness, forgotten and deserted, in death and nothingness. They suffer distresses and miseries without knowing where to find relief. Keeping their eyes toward heaven alone, they wait peacefully and without fear for help to come. And God, who seeks no purer disposition in his loved ones than this entire surrender of self-interest in order to live by grace and divine operation alone, provides them with the necessary books, thoughts, self-understanding, advice, and wise counsel. Everything that others discover by diligent searching, these souls find in self-surrender. What others store up with care so they can find it again, these souls receive the very moment there is need of it, and afterward they relinquish it again, taking only what God is willing to give, in order to live through him alone.

Others undertake an infinity of good works for the glory of God, but these souls are often cast aside in a corner of the world like bits of broken crockery, apparently of no use to anyone. There these souls, forsaken by humankind but enjoying God with a very real, true, and passionate, though deeply tranquil, love, attempt nothing by their own impulse. They know only that they must surrender themselves and remain in God's hands to be used by him as he pleases. Often they do not know of what use they might be, but God knows well. The world considers them of no account, but it is nonetheless true that in mysterious ways and through hidden channels these souls spread abroad an infinite amount of grace on persons who often are unaware of them, people of whom these souls may themselves be unaware.

In these surrendered souls everything effectively preaches the good news of the gospel. God gives their silence, their quiet, their self-forgetfulness, their words, and their gestures a certain virtue, which, unknown to themselves, works in the hearts of those around them. And, just as they are guided by the random actions of innumerable creatures that are unknowingly influenced by grace, they themselves, in their turn, are used to support and guide others without any direct acquaintance with them or knowledge that this is what they are doing.

It is God who works in them in unforeseen and often unknown impulses. In this way they are like Jesus, from whom went out a secret power for the healing of others. There is this difference between him and them: often they are not conscious of the outflow of this power and contribute nothing by way of cooperation. It is like a hidden aromatic preparation, a healing ointment that people perceive without recognizing, and which is itself unaware of its own healing virtue.

CHAPTER 2

The More Excellent Way

When souls discover this divine influence, they leave aside all their good works, practices of devotion, methods, books, ideas, and spiritual persons in order to be guided by God alone, entrusting themselves to the purpose that has become the only source of perfection for them. They are in his hand as saints have always been, understanding that he alone can guide them in the right path, and that if they were to search for other means, they would inevitably be led astray in that land of the unknown in which God calls them to walk. It is therefore God's mysterious action in them that guides and leads them by ways that only he knows.

With them, it is something like changes of the wind. The direction can be known only in the present moment. Whatever they do instinctively or by the duty of their circumstance can be known as a leading of God only by its results. This is the only spirituality they know. These are their visions and revelations, the whole of their wisdom and counsel, insomuch that nothing is ever lacking to them. Faith gives them assurance that what they do is good, whether they read, speak, or write.

And if these souls take counsel, it is only to be able to distinguish more clearly what God's will is. They accept this as a part of God's order, and look for his influence underneath what is said, rather than concentrating on the particulars themselves. Their decision to use or discount such counsel they always make by faith, leaning on the infallible, unruffled, unchangeable, and ever-effective presence of God. Thus they perceive and enjoy God's presence in everything, the least as well as the greatest, finding it always available at every moment. In this way they make use of things, not because they have any confidence in them, or for their own sake, but in obedience to God's will and the reality of his presence, which they discern with equal certainty and ease, in spite of all appearances to the contrary. And so their life is not spent in questions, vain wishes, weariness, or sighs, but in the continual assurance that they possess what is most perfect.

They endure every state of the body and soul. Whatever happens to them internally or externally as each moment brings it to them contains the fullness of God's active presence and becomes their joy. The whole of creation is for them nothing but misery and deprivation, since the only true and just measure of things is the fulfillment of God's purpose. So, if his will should mean the taking away of thoughts, words, books, food, companions, health, even life itself, it is exactly the same as if it should mean the opposite. These souls love God's will and find it equally sanctifying, no matter in what shape it comes. They do not speculate about the way God's will comes to pass; it is enough that they know the Source to give their assent to whatever comes.

CHAPTER 3

Pure Faith, Hope, and Love

The state of full surrender is a certain combination of faith, hope, and love in one single action that unites the soul to God and his will. United, these three virtues together form one single act, the raising of our hearts to God and our surrender to his divine work.

But how can this divine combination, this spiritual oneness be explained? How can a name be found to convey an idea of its nature and to make the unity of these three intelligible? It can be explained like this: it is only by means of these three virtues that we can possess God and enjoy his will. The beloved object is seen, is loved, and all things are hoped for from it. Any of these virtues can with equal justice be called pure love, pure hope, or pure faith. If this state of which we are speaking is more frequently called "pure faith," it is not because hope and love have been excluded. Rather, it is that all these virtues are practiced in a hidden way in this state.

On God's side, nothing can be more secure than this state; as far as the human heart is concerned, nothing is freer from selfish motive or interest. From God comes the certainty of faith, and on the heart's side, that same certainty is tempered with fear and hope. How desirable is the unity-in-trinity of these three holy virtues! Then believe, hope, and love, but do so by the simple touch that the God-given Holy Spirit produces in your heart. In this touch is the anointing oil of the name of God with which the Holy Spirit anoints you in the depths of your heart. That is the word of promise, the mystical revelation, and a pledge of the happiness that God has prepared for us. "Truly God is good to the upright, to those who are pure in heart" (Psalm 73:1).

This touch in souls that are on fire with God's love is called pure love because of the torrent of delight overflowing every faculty, accompanied by an abundance of confidence and illumination. But in souls that are plunged in bitterness, it is called pure faith, because they see nothing but darkness and the obscurity of night. Pure love sees, feels, and believes. Pure faith believes without either seeing or feeling. That is the difference between these two states, but it is only an apparent, not a real difference. Although they seem different, in reality, the state of pure faith is not lacking in love, and the state of pure love never lacks faith or surrender of self. The terms apply according to which virtue prevails. The different mixtures of these virtues, under the touch of the Holy Spirit, form the variety of all supernatural and transcendent spiritual experiences. And since God is able to blend them in an endless variety, there is not a single soul who does not receive its touch in a way completely suitable to it, always with the same ingredients: faith, hope, and love.

Surrender of self is the universal means of receiving special virtues in every variety of these impressions of the Holy Spirit. Different souls cannot lay claim to the same mixture of virtues, or to the same experience that others have, but all can be united to God, all can be surrendered to his holy purpose, all can receive the touch best suited for them. All, in fact, can live under the reign of God and enjoy a share in his kingdom with all its blessings. In this kingdom every soul can aspire to a crown, and whether it is a crown of love or a crown of faith, it is always a crown, always the kingdom of God. There is this difference, it is true—earthly crowns bring honor and fame, while the crowns given in the kingdom of God lead to obscurity. But again, what does this matter if the soul belongs to God and obeys his will? We do not seek to know the name of this state, its specific distinctions, or its degree of excellence. No, we seek God alone and his purpose. The way in which that is brought to pass should be a matter of indifference to us.

Let us not preach about the state of pure love or of perfect faith, the way of delights, or the way of the cross, for these cannot be imparted to all in the same degree or the same manner. Let us rather preach surrender to God's will, to all the pure in heart who fear God, and let us make them understand that by this surrender they will attain to whatever particular state has been chosen and planned for them by God's purpose from all eternity.

Let us not dishearten anyone, or rebuff, or drive anyone away from that highest perfection to which Jesus calls everyone. For Jesus requires that all people everywhere submit to the will of his heavenly Father and be made members of his mystical body. He is truly their Master only insofar as their will is in accord with his. Let us continually repeat to all souls that the invitation of their sweet and loving Savior does not demand anything very difficult or extraordinary from them. He does not ask for talent and ingenuity. All he asks is that their wills be united to him, so that he may guide, lead, and befriend them accordingly.

CHAPTER 4

The Joy of Full Surrender

There is nothing freer than a heart that sees only the life of God in the most deadly perils and troubles. Even when it is a question of drinking poison, standing in the breach during a battle, or slaving for people stricken by the plague, it finds in its circumstances a veritable abundance of divine life, not given by drops, but in floods that overwhelm and engulf the soul in an instant.

If an army were animated by the same ideals, it would be invincible, because the moving power of faith lifts and enlarges the heart above and beyond anything the senses can experience.

The life of faith and the moving power of faith are exactly the same. Such a life is an enjoyment of God's gift, and a confidence grounded in the expectation of his protection, making everything pleasant and enabling us to receive everything with good grace. It works a kind of indifference to varying states of life, locations, or companionships. Yet, at the same time, it prepares us for all of them. Faith is never unhappy, even when the senses are the most wretched. This lively faith is always in God, always in his overarching providential action, in spite of any contrary appearances to the senses. The senses, in terror, suddenly cry to the soul, "Unhappy one! You have no resource left; you are lost!" Instantly faith with a stronger voice answers: "Keep firm, go forward, and fear nothing!"

CHAPTER 5

The Great Worth of Pure Faith

Whatever we find extraordinary in the lives of the saints—revelations, visions, inner movements—they are only glimpses of that real excellence of their condition contained and hidden in the exercise of faith. This is because faith possesses all this simply by knowing how to see and hear God in what happens from moment to moment. When such favors are manifested visibly it does not mean that they have not already been possessed by faith. Rather it is to make faith's excellence visible so that others will be attracted to the practice of it, just as the glory of Jesus Christ on the Mount of Transfiguration and his miracles did not come from any increase of his intrinsic excellence, but from the light that escaped from time to time from the dark cloud of his humanity to make it an object of worship and love to others.

What is wonderful in the saints is their constancy of faith under every circumstance. Without this there would be no saintliness. In the loving faith that causes them to rejoice in God for everything, their holiness does not need any extraordinary manifestation. Its usefulness lies in its benefit to others who might need the confirmation of such signs. But the soul in this state, happy in its obscurity, in no way relies on these brilliant manifestations. It allows them to show outwardly for the sake of others, but keeps for itself what all have in common: the will of God and his good pleasure. The saint's faith is proved in hiding itself, not showing itself, and those who require more proof have less faith.

Those who live by faith receive proofs, not as such, but as favors from the hand of God, and in this sense there is no contradiction between these extraordinary manifestations and pure faith. But there are many saints whom God raises up for the salvation of others, from whose faces he causes rays of glory to stream to enlighten even the blindest. Such were the prophets and the apostles and all those saints chosen by God and set, so to speak, on a lampstand, to give light to all in the house. There have always been saints like these and there always will be.

There is also a multitude of others in the Church who are hidden and who, having been created to shine only in heaven, shed no light in this life, but live and die in complete obscurity.

CHAPTER 6
Surrender Is Everything

Surrender of the heart to God includes every possible way of obedience to God, because it means giving up one's very being to God's good pleasure. Since this surrender is accomplished by unalloyed love, it includes in its embrace every kind of operation his good pleasure may bring to pass. Thus at every moment we practice a surrender that has no limits, a surrender that includes all possible methods and degrees of service to God. It is not our business to decide what the ultimate purpose of such submission may be, but our sole duty is to submit ourselves to all that God sends us and to stand ready to do his will at all times.

What God requires of the soul is the essence of self-surrender. The free gifts he asks from us are self-denial, obedience, and love. The rest is his business. It does not matter whether the soul is carefully fulfilling the duties of our state in life, or quietly following the leadings it is given, or submitting peacefully to the dealings of grace either to the body or to the soul. In all this, the soul is exercising within the one overall act of self-surrender. It is not a matter of single, isolated incidents or the duty of one moment, but the act always carries with it the full merit and good effect that a sincere good will always has, although the outcome does not depend on the single act of surrender. What the soul desires to do is done as in the sight of God.

If it happens that God's will sets a limit to the exercise of some particular faculty of ours, he sets no limit on our wills. The good pleasure of God, God's being and essence are the objects of the will, and through the exercise of love it is united with God without limit, manner, or measure. If this love results in the exercise of only one faculty or another for a certain object, this means that the will of God goes only so far: it contracts itself, so to speak, restricting itself to the specific needs of the moment, engaging the faculties and then going on into the heart. Finding the heart pure, untrammeled, and holding nothing back, God communicates his will fully to it, because his love has given it an infinite capacity by emptying it of all created things and making it capable of union with God.

Heavenly purity! Blessed Emptying! Unreserved submission! Through these, God is welcomed into the very center of the heart! It matters not what my abilities may be then, provided that I possess you, Lord. Do what you will with this insignificant creature. Whether I should work, or become inspired, or be the recipient of your impressions, it is all the same. Everything is yours, everything is from you and for you. I no longer have anything to be concerned about, anything to do. I have no hand in the arrangement of one single moment of my life. Everything belongs to you. I do not need to add or subtract anything, or to search after or mull over anything. It is for you, Lord, to regulate everything: direction, humiliations, means of making us holy, perfection, salvation—all are your business, Lord. Mine is to be satisfied with your work and not to demand the choice of action or condition, but to leave everything to your good pleasure.

CHAPTER 7

Enjoying the Blessings of Surrender

It is self-surrender that I preach, God, and not any particular condition of life. Every condition in which your grace places a soul is the same to me. I teach people a means of getting to the condition that you have marked out for them. I would not exact more from them than the will to surrender themselves to your guidance. You will make them arrive infallibly at the condition that is best for them.

It is faith that I proclaim, Lord: surrender, confidence, and trust. The will must be submitted to and be the instrument of your divine purpose, and I believe that this purpose is being worked out at every moment, in every circumstance, according to our degree of willingness. That is the faith I preach. It is not a special kind of faith or love, but a universal state in which all souls can find God under the different ways he comes to them, and whatever conditions his grace allots for them.

I have already spoken to souls in trouble. I am speaking now to all kinds of souls. It is my heart's desire to care for everyone, to proclaim the saving secret far and wide, and to make myself all things to all people. In this happy frame of heart, I make it a duty to weep with those who weep, to rejoice with those who rejoice, to speak simply to the unlearned, and with the learned to make use of the most learned and scholastic terms. I want to make everyone understand that although we cannot aspire to the same special favors, we can attain to the same love, the same self-denial, the same God and his work, and from this it follows naturally that we can attain to the greatest degree of saintliness. What are called extraordinary graces given as privileges to certain souls are only so called because there are so few who are faithful enough to be able to receive them. This will be made manifest at the day of judgment. How woeful it is that it will then be seen that instead of God's having withheld such divine favors, it has been entirely our own fault that we have been deprived of them. What untold blessings would we have received through the complete submission of a steady will!

The same applies in regard to Jesus as with God's divine purpose. If those who have no faith in him or respect for him receive none of the favors he offers to everyone, they have only themselves to blame. It is true that we cannot all aspire to the same sublime states, the same gifts, even the same degree of perfection. Yet, if we were faithful to the grace we have, if we acted according to the measure of it, we would all be satisfied, because we would all attain that degree of grace and perfection that would fully satisfy us. We would then be happy according to nature and according to grace, because nature and grace share equally in their ardent desire for this priceless advantage of unity with God.

CHAPTER 8
The Treasury of Grace

Therefore, those who wish to enjoy an abundance of all blessings have to do just one thing: purify their hearts by weaning them away from all creatures and surrender themselves entirely to God. In this purity and surrender they will find all they desire.

Lord, let others ask you for all sorts of gifts; let them multiply their words and prayers. As for me, dearest God, I ask only one gift. I have only one prayer to make: give me a pure heart.

You who are pure of heart, how happy you are! For by the liveliness of your faith you see God as he is in himself. You see him in all things and at every moment at work within you and around you. In everything you are God's subject and his instrument. He rules you and leads you. You do not have to think because he thinks for you. Whatever happens to you, or may happen by his will, it is enough for him that you desire it also. He understands your readiness. In your blindness you try to find this desire in yourself, but you cannot. Yet he sees it quite clearly. How foolish you are! A well-disposed heart is a heart in which God dwells. Seeing the good inclinations in such a heart, God knows well that it will ever remain submissive to his will. He knows, too, that you are ignorant of what would be useful to you, and therefore he makes it his business to give you what is best.

It matters very little to him whether you are thwarted or not. You imagine you are going east, and he makes you go west. You are about to strike a reef; he pushes the tiller and brings you into port. With neither map nor compass, wind, or tide, your voyages are always successful. If you meet pirates, an unexpected puff of wind instantly wafts you beyond their reach.

A good will! A pure heart! How well did Jesus know where to put them when he placed them among the Beatitudes! What greater happiness can there be than to possess God and be possessed by him? It is a state full of charm and of joy, in which the soul reposes peacefully in the bosom of divine Providence, where it plays with divine Wisdom like a child, feeling no anxiety about the journey that continues without interruption past rocks and pirates and storms, ever continuing on its happy way.

A pure heart! A good will! The sole foundation of every spiritual state! To such a heart are given the gifts of firm faith, holy hope, perfect trust, and pure love.

On this stem are grafted the flowers of the desert. In other words, from such a heart spring those priceless graces that bloom in souls that are entirely detached, where God takes up his abode, as in an empty house, to the exclusion of everything else. The pure heart is the bountiful, plentiful source from which come streams to water the garden of the divine Lord and his chosen one. Its voice calls to every soul, saying, "Look well at me: it is I who impart fair love, the love that chooses the better part and lays hold of it. It is I who give birth to that fear, so gentle and powerful, that produces a horror of evil and makes it easy to avoid. It is I who bring the knowledge that discloses the greatness of God and the value of virtue. It is from me that those fervent desires rise to enkindle holy hope. It is I who cause virtue to be practiced while awaiting the possession of that divine Object of your love that is now the joy and will one day be the even greater happiness of faithful souls."

Such a pure heart can invite everyone to come to it to be enriched from its inexhaustible treasures. All spiritual conditions and paths lead back to purity of heart. From it they all derive what is beautiful, attractive, and charming, drawing their beauty from its depths. Those wonderful fruits of grace and all kinds of virtue that nourish the soul, abounding on every side, come from the pure heart. Milk and honey flow abundantly here.

Let us go, then, beloved, let us fly to that ocean of love that draws us! What are we waiting for? Let us start at once; let us lose ourselves in God, in his very heart, to become intoxicated with the wine of his love! We shall find in his heart the key of heavenly treasures. Let us begin our journey to heaven at once. There is no path we cannot explore. Nothing is closed to us—not the garden, the cellar, or the vineyard. If we desire to breathe the fresh country air, we can direct our steps there and return when we please. With this key of David we can go in and out. It is the key of knowledge and of that deep storehouse in which are contained all the hidden treasures of divine Wisdom. With this heavenly key we also open the gates of mystical death and its sacred darkness. By it we descend into the deep pools and into the lions' den. By it we are thrust into those obscure prisons from which we emerge unscathed. By it we are introduced into that joyful place where light and understanding dwell, where the Bridegroom takes his noonday rest in the open air, and where he reveals the secrets of his love to faithful souls, heavenly secrets that no mortal tongue can describe!

Let us love then, dear friends, since every good thing that it is possible to give is given to those who love. For love produces saintliness with all that goes with it. It flows in from every side into the hearts open to receive its divine outpouring. Divine harvest for eternity—it is not possible to praise it enough! But why should we speak about it? How much better to possess it in silence than to praise it with mere words! But what am I saying? God must be praised, but only because he has taken hold of us, for from the moment his love enters our heart, then reading, writing, speaking, or silence are all the same.

We can take or leave anything—live in solitude or as a messenger sent to teach others; be well or ill, dull or eloquent— anything at all. That which love dictates, the heart, love's faithful echo, repeats to all the other faculties of the soul. Divine Love regards that mixture of matter and spirit, the heart, as its own kingdom. There love reigns supreme. Since the heart has no other inclinations but what Love inspires, all the things that are presented to it are equally agreeable. Such things as nature or the devil would substitute cause nothing but disgust and horror. If God should occasionally allow the heart to be overcome by such things, it is only to make it wiser and more humble. But from the moment it realizes its mistake, it returns to God with more love and clings to him with even greater faithfulness.

BOOK III

GOD'S FATHERLY CARE OF THOSE WHO PRACTICE SELF-SURRENDER

Sacrifice: The Foundation of Spiritual Life

Offer right sacrifices, says the prophet, *and put your trust in the LORD* (Psalm 4:5). That is to say that the great and solid foundation of our spiritual life is to give ourselves to God, being subject to his good pleasure in all things, both inwardly and outwardly. It means to forget ourselves so completely that we regard ourselves as sold and delivered, as having no more right to ourselves. In this way our joy and happiness consist wholly in the good pleasure of God, and his favor and glory and being form our only contentment.

Having laid this foundation, we have nothing else to do but to rejoice that God is God, and surrender ourselves so entirely to his good pleasure that we feel an equal satisfaction whatever his will calls for, never pausing to wonder about the use he makes of us.

To surrender our *selves!* This, then, is our principal duty that remains to be lived after we have fulfilled faithfully all the responsibilities of our state of life. The degree to which we perform this principal duty is the degree of our holiness.

A saintly person is none other than a person who is surrendered, by God's grace, to God's divine will. All that follows this free submission is the work of God, not of human beings. God asks nothing more than that we should receive what he sends us without demanding to see or understand, no matter what it may be. This is all that God requires of us, and as to the rest, he determines and chooses according to his own plans, as an architect selects and arranges stones for the building he is about to construct.

We should, then, love God and his will in everything, and love this will in whatever way it is made known to us, without desiring anything else. It is for God, not for us, to determine the conditions of our submission, and whatever he sends is best for our souls. The whole of the spiritual life can be condensed into this word: we should submit ourselves entirely to God's overruling, and by continually forgetting ourselves, we should be totally occupied in loving and serving him, free of fears, reflections, vain regrets, and anxieties, which so often occupy those who are worried about their own salvation and perfection. Since God offers to take our cares upon himself, let us place everything in his hands once and for all, leaving them to his infinite wisdom, so that we may concern ourselves no more with anything but him.

Go forward, then, my soul, with head uplifted above earthly things, always content with God, content with what he does with us and with what he gives us to do. Take good care not to foolishly entertain a crowd of anxious reflections, which, like so many tangled labyrinths, entrap the mind into useless, endless wanderings. Let us avoid this snare of self-love by leaping over it, not following its interminable windings.

Onward, my soul, through weariness, sickness, times of dryness, flares of temper, weaknesses of mind, the snares of the devil and of other people; through suspicions, jealousies, evil imaginations, and prejudices! Let us soar like the eagle above all these clouds with eyes always fixed on the sun and on its rays of light, which represent our obligations. Doubtless we may feel these trials. It is not for us to be insensitive to them, but let us remember that our life is not a life of feeling. Let us live in the higher regions of the soul where God and his will form an eternity, where there is no variation or shadow due to change.

In this wholly spiritual dwelling the Uncreated, the Inexpressible and Infinite holds the soul apart from every specific shadow and situation, and keeps it in perpetual calm, even though the senses are tossed about by tempests. We have learned to rise above the senses. Their restlessness, their agitations and innumerable changes disturb us no more than clouds that darken the sky for a moment and disappear. We know that in the region of the senses, all things are like clouds blown along by the wind, without sequence or order, but always in a state of perpetual change.

In the state of faith, God's will forms the eternal charm of the heart, just as it will be its eternal and true happiness in the state of glory, and this glorious state of the heart will shed its influence throughout our material being, which now finds itself a prey to terrors and temptations. Beneath these monstrous forms, terrible though they may be, the activity of God will give our whole being a heavenly power that will cause it to shine like the sun. For the faculties of the responsive soul and those of the body are being prepared here below, like gold or iron, or like canvas for a picture, or stones for a building. And like these different substances, they will attain their purity and splendor of form only when they have passed through many changes and suffered many losses, and have survived many destructions. Whatever we endure here at the hand of God is intended as a preparation for our future state.

In the state of faith, the soul that knows the secret of God always dwells in perfect peace. All that happens within, rather than alarming it, reassures it. Deeply convinced that it is God who guides it, it takes all that happens as so much grace, and overlooking the means God uses for his work, the soul thinks only of the work he is doing.

The faithful soul is moved to action by love to fulfill faithfully and exactly all its duties. All that such a surrendered soul apprehends distinctly is God's work of grace, with the exception of those sins that are slight and that grace even turns to a good account. I use the term "apprehends distinctly" to apply to all those impressions made by the will of God in the soul, either of sorrow or of consolation, that are given for the soul's good. I use the term "distinct" because, of all that goes on in the soul, these impressions are what it understands best. In all these things, faith sees only God, and applies itself solely to being conformed to his will.

CHAPTER 2

The Pains and Consolations of Surrender to God

The state of full surrender is full of consolation for those who have reached it, but in order to reach it we must pass through much anguish. The truth of pure love is learned only by the action of God upon the soul, not by any effort of the mind. God teaches the heart by pains and obstacles, not by ideas.

This knowledge is the knowledge of experience, by which God is enjoyed as the only good. In order to master this knowledge, we must be detached from all personal possessions, and to gain this detachment, we must in reality be deprived of them. It is therefore only by constant crosses, and by a long succession of all kinds of mortifications, trials, and deprivations, that pure love becomes established in our souls. This must continue until all created things become to us as though they did not exist, and God becomes all in all.

To accomplish this, God combats all the particular affections of the heart, so that when the heart is led to some particular idea of piety, or some special help to devotion, or when there is any idea of being able to reach perfection by some such method, or by such a path or way, or by the guidance of some particular person—in short, to whatever the heart fixes itself, God upsets its plans, and allows it to find, instead of success in these projects, nothing but confusion, trouble, emptiness, and folly. Hardly have we said, "I must go this way; I must consult this person; or, I must act in this manner," than God immediately says the exact opposite, and withdraws all the power that is usually present in the means that we have just decided to use. So, finding only deception and utter emptiness in everything, we are compelled to have recourse to God himself and to be content with him.

Happy is the soul that understands this loving severity of God and cooperates with it faithfully. Such a person is raised above all that passes away, to rest in the unchanging and the infinite. We are no longer scattered aimlessly among created things by giving them love and confidence, but the soul gives them entrance only when it becomes a duty to do so, or by God's command, and when it is especially shown that this is God's will. The heart dwells in a region above earthly abundance or poverty, in the fullness of God who is its permanent good. God finds such a soul quite free of its own inclinations, of its own movements, of its own choice. It is a dead subject, and shrouded in total impartiality.

The wholeness of the Living God, coming in this way to fill the heart, casts over everything else a shadow, a kind of emptiness, making all distinctions and varieties irrelevant. Thus there remains neither efficacy nor virtue in any created thing, and the heart has neither drawing nor inclination toward them, because the majesty of God fills it so completely. Living in God in this way, the heart becomes dead to everything else, and everything is dead to it. It is for God, who gives life to all things, to cause the heart to be enlivened with regard to any created thing, and to enliven created things with regard to the soul. God's will is that life. By God's will, the heart goes out toward created things as far as is necessary or useful, and by his will other creatures are attracted to the heart and are accepted by it. Without this divine power of God's good pleasure at work, the faithful heart does not welcome created things and is not attracted to them. This dissolving of all created things into nothingness and bringing them back at the point of God's will, causes the soul at every moment to look for God himself in everything that happens. Each moment is both contentment with God alone in one's heart and total self-surrender to every possible created thing or circumstance that might come according to God's will. In this way, every moment contains the completeness of our total surrender to him.

CHAPTER 3
Regarding Rules and Inspirations

Those who are called to this fullness of surrender, although they are more passive than active in heart, cannot expect to be exempted from all activity. This fullness of surrender is nothing else but surrender to God practiced more habitually and more completely, and should consist of two kinds of duty: actively accomplishing God's will, and passively accepting all that his will is pleased to send us.

It consists essentially, as we have already said, of giving our whole self to God to be used as he pleases. Now the good pleasure of God makes use of us in two ways: either it compels us to perform certain actions, or it simply works within us. We submit also in two ways: either by faithfully carrying out his clearly understood commands, or else by simply and passively submitting to his impressions on our hearts, either of pleasure or pain. Surrender implies all this, since it is nothing but perfect submission to God's will made clear in the present moment. It matters little to the soul what the manner of this submission must be, or what the present moment may contain. But it is absolutely important to it to give itself up completely.

There are prescribed duties to be fulfilled and necessary duties to be accepted. And further, there is a third kind that also forms part of active faithfulness, although it does not fall into the category of a rule of behavior. This third kind we may call "inspired duties": those to which the Spirit of God inclines the hearts that are submissive to him. Accomplishing this kind of duty requires great simplicity of heart, a gentle and cheerful disposition, a heart easily moved by every breath of directing grace. For there is nothing to do but to give ourselves up and obey such inspirations freely and simply. So that our souls may not be deceived, God always gives us wise guidance to indicate with what liberty or reserve we should make use of such inspirations.

This third kind of duty takes precedence over all law, formalities, or laid-out rules. It is what appears extraordinary and spectacular in the lives of the saints. It is what regulates their spoken prayer, their interior words, their feelings, and all that makes their lives noble, such as their austerities, their zeal, and their extravagant self-sacrifice for others. Since all this belongs to the interior reign of the Holy Spirit, no one should try to obtain it, to imagine that they have it, to desire it, or to regret that they are not given the grace to undertake this kind of work or practice the uncommon virtues of the saints, because they are really of any value or merit only when they are done according to the direction of God. If we are not content with this reserve, we lay ourselves open to the influence of our own ideas and become exposed to illusion.

We should remark that there are souls whom God keeps hidden and little in their own eyes and in the eyes of others. Far from giving them any striking qualities, his design for them is that they should remain in obscurity. They would deceive themselves if they attempted a different way. If they are taught well, they will recognize that faithfulness to their own nothingness is the right path for them, and they will find peace in their lowliness. Therefore, the only difference, in their way and that of others who appear more favored, is the difference they make for themselves by the amount of love and surrender they have to the will of God. For, if in love and self-surrender they surpass the souls that appear to accomplish more outwardly than they, their saintliness is, without doubt, so much the greater. This shows that each of us should content ourselves with the duties of our state, and with the overruling of Providence. Clearly God requires this equally of everyone.

As for leadings and impressions received by the soul, these are given by God alone to whom he pleases. We must not try to produce them ourselves or make efforts to increase them. Natural effort is in direct opposition and quite contrary to true inspirations, which should come in peace. The voice of the Bridegroom should awaken the soul, which should then proceed only according to the inspirations of the Holy Spirit, for otherwise, it will make no progress.

Therefore, if we feel neither a leading of the Spirit nor the grace to do those things that are so admired in the saints, we must in all fairness to ourselves say, "God has willed it to be so for the saints, but not for me."

CHAPTER 4
A Direct and Safe Way

Those who are called by God to live in perfect self-surrender are in this respect like our Lord, his holy Mother, and St. Joseph. God's will was the whole of life to them. Submitting entirely to this will as their rule and inspiration as soon as it was made known to them, they were always in complete dependence on what we might call "the purely providential will of God." It follows from this that their lives, although extraordinary in perfection, showed outwardly only that which was common and quite ordinary. They fulfilled the duties of religion and of their state as others do, and apparently in the same way. As for the rest, if we look carefully at their way of life, we can discover nothing either striking or peculiar. Everything follows the normal course of ordinary events. Anything that would single them out is not discernable. It is rather dependence on the supreme will that arranges everything for them and in which they habitually live. God's will confers on them a complete self-mastery because of the constant submission of their hearts.

These fully surrendered souls are both solitary and free because of their spiritual state. They are detached from all things in order to belong to God, to love him in peace, and to fulfill faithfully their present duty according to his expressed will. They do not allow themselves to reflect, to put off, or to worry about the consequences, the causes, or the reasons for such duties. It is enough for them to go on simply doing their plain duties. It is just as if nothing else existed for them but God and their duty of the moment.

The present moment, then, is like a desert in which the soul sees only God in whom it delights. And it is occupied only about those things that he requires of it, leaving and forgetting all else, and abandoning it to Providence. This soul, like an instrument, neither receives inwardly more than God's operation brings about, nor acts beyond what that same operation causes.

This inward action of God receives the soul's full and free cooperation, yet it is something that the soul receives from outside itself in a mystical way. That is to say that as God finds in such a soul all the necessary conditions that enable it to act according to his laws, and is satisfied with its good will, he then spares it the trouble of any self-generated action, giving it all that would otherwise be the fruit of its own effort or of its effective goodwill. It is as though someone, seeing a friend preparing for a journey, could somehow put his own strength and power into the friend, and under the appearance of his friend would undertake the journey using his own energy, so that the friend would need to have only the will to walk, while in reality it was done by the strength of another. This journey would be free because it would be the result of a free decision taken beforehand to please the friend, who then takes upon himself the trouble and the expense. It would also be active because it would really be taken. Yet it would be inward, because it was accomplished without outward activity on the soul's part. Finally, it would be mystical, because of the hidden principle contained in it.

But to return to the kind of cooperation we have explained by this imaginary journey: observe that it is entirely different from faithfulness in the fulfillment of obligations. The work of fulfilling these neither is mystical nor comes from outside ourselves, but is free and active in the ordinary understanding of these words. The full surrender of oneself to the will of God has both activity and passivity in it. There is nothing of self in it, but a constant goodwill, which, like an instrument, has no action of itself, but responds to the touch of the master. While it is in his hands it fulfills all the purposes for which it was made.

On the other hand, intentional and determined obedience to the will of God is part of the ordinary order of vigilance, care, attention, prudence, and discretion, although, of course, all our ordinary efforts are aided and inspired by grace. Everything else we should leave to God, reserving for ourselves at the present moment only love and obedience, which we will practice through all eternity.

This love, infused into the soul in silence, is a true act of the soul, evoking a perpetual obligation to preserve it. We cannot do this without acting out the impulses that come from it. These actions, however, are quite different from obedience to our present duty. We should so dispose all our faculties to fulfill God's will in the present moment as it is shown to us outwardly, without expecting anything extraordinary.

To the soul God's will is in all things its method, its rule, and its direct and safe way. His will is an unalterable law that belongs to all times, all places, and all states. It is a straight line that the soul must follow with courage and faithfulness, neither veering to the right or the left nor overstepping the bounds. Whatever is given over and above this must be received and carried out in disregard of oneself. In a word, we are to be active in all that the present duty requires, but submissive and unresistant to all the rest, without self-will, patiently waiting for the moving of God's will.

CHAPTER 5

The Common Way of All Saints

It is by union with God's will that we enjoy and possess him. It is an illusion to try to obtain this heavenly enjoyment in any other way. The will of God is the universal way. It does not belong only to one method. All methods and all ways are made holy by it. God's will brings God to our souls in many different ways, and that by which he is brought to us is always best for us. We should esteem and love them all, because in each of them we should see God's will accommodating itself to each individual soul, selecting the most suitable method of bringing about its union with him. Our duty is to submit to this choice and make none for ourselves, and to do this without exempting ourselves from adoring, esteeming, and loving his will as it works in others.

For example, if God's will should direct me toward saying vocal prayers, toward a sense of devotion, or toward special understanding of great mysteries, I should still love and esteem silence and bareness in the lives of others. For myself, I should make use of the duty of the present moment and by it should become united to God. I should not (as the Quietists do), reduce all religion to personal inaction, despising all other means. What makes perfection is obedience to God's law, which always adapts the means it uses to exactly fit the soul. No, I should not admit roadblocks or limits to the will of God, nor should I take anything in its place, but welcome it in whatever way it is made known to me. And I should revere it in whatever way it is pleased to come to others.

Thus all ordinary souls have but one common way, yet distinct and different for each one, in order to form the variety of the mystical robe of the Church. All souls who are simple in heart mutually approve of and esteem each other, and say, "Let us go toward the same goal by different paths, united in the same way and by the same means in the kingdom of God, which is so different in each one of us." It is in this sense that we must read the lives of the saints and other spiritual books, without ever being detoured, and without forsaking our own path. For this reason, we should not read spiritual books or hold spiritual conversations with others unless God wills it. If he makes such readings or conversations the duty of the present moment, instead of causing any detour, we will be strengthened in the way laid out for us, either by what we find in conformity with our own method or even by that in which we differ. But if the will of God does not make this reading or spiritual exchange a present duty, it will cause nothing but trouble and confusion, because without the concurrence of God's will, there can be no order in anything.

How long indeed have we busied ourselves with pains and anxieties that have nothing to do with our present duty! When will God be all in all to us? Let others act according to their nature, but let nothing hinder us. Let us go beyond all created things and live entirely for God.

CHAPTER 6

The Obedient Heart

We must detach ourselves from all that we feel or do if we are to walk in this way with God, living only in God and the duty of the present moment. We must disregard anything beyond this as being superfluous. We must restrict ourselves to the present duty without thinking about the one just past or the one just ahead.

I take for granted, of course, that the law of God is always before you and the practice of joyful surrender has made your soul easily influenced by the movement of God within. You feel some impulse that makes you say, "I have a drawing toward this person," or "I have an inclination to read a certain book, to receive or to give certain counsel, or to receive some confidence, or to give something away or to perform some action." Obey this impulse that comes from the inspiration of grace without stopping to reflect, reason, or delay. Give yourself up to these things for as long as God wills without letting any self-will intrude. In this state of surrender we are describing, the will of God is shown to us because he dwells within us. His revealed will should take the place of all our usual supports.

Every moment brings its own duty to be practiced. The obedient soul is faithful to it. Nothing that has been learned by reading or hearing is forgotten, and the lowliest novice could not fulfill his or her duties better. It is for this reason that such surrendered souls are attracted sometimes to one book, sometimes to another, or are led to make some remark or some reflection on what may seem only a trifling circumstance. At one moment God gives the leading to learn something that at a later moment will encourage them in the doing of their duty.

Whatever these persons do, they do it because they are led to do it, without knowing why. All they can explain on the subject can be reduced to this: "I feel myself led to write, to read, to ask, to look into that. I follow this leading and God who gives it to me keeps these things, so to speak, in reserve in my subconscious, to become in the future a kind of nucleus of other leadings that will become useful to myself and others." This is what makes it so necessary for these people to be gentle, yielding and submissive to the faintest breath of these scarcely perceptible "nudges."

In this state of joyful self-surrender, the only rule is the present moment. In this our soul is as light as a feather, liquid as water, simple as a child, as easily moved as a ball in following these nudges of grace. Such persons have no more consistency and rigidity than molten metal. As such metal takes any form according to the mold into which it is poured, so these souls are pliant and easily shaped to any form that God chooses to give them. In a word, their disposition resembles the air, which is affected by every breeze, or water, which flows into any vessel, whatever shape it may be, and fills every crevice. Before God they are like a smoothly woven canvas, neither thinking nor trying to know what God will be pleased to paint on it, because they have confidence in him. They give themselves to him, and since they are entirely taken up with what he gives them to do, they do not think of themselves or of what they may need or how to obtain it.

The more enthusiastically they apply themselves to their humble handiwork, which is so simple, so hidden, so secret, and outwardly unimportant, the more God embroiders and embellishes it with brilliant colors. On the surface of this smooth canvas of love and obedience, his hand traces the most beautiful design, the most delicate and intricate pattern, the most divine figures. *The* LORD *has set apart the faithful for himself* (Psalm 4:3). It is true that a smooth and blank canvas given up to the work of the brush feels at each moment only the one single brushstroke. Each blow of the hammer on the chisel can produce only one cruel mark at a time, and the stone that is struck by repeated blows cannot know or see the form the blows are producing. It feels only that it is being diminished, filed, cut, and disfigured by the chisel. A stone that is destined to become a crucifix or a statue without knowing it, if asked, "What is happening to you?" would reply if it could speak, "Don't ask me! I only know one thing, and that is to remain immovable in the hands of my master, to love him and to endure all that he inflicts on me. As for what I am destined to be and how to achieve it, that is his business. I am as ignorant of what he is doing as I am of what I am destined to become. All I know is that his work is the best, the most perfect that it could be, and I receive each blow of the chisel as the best thing that could happen to me, although, in truth, it feels to me that each blow brings ruin, destruction, and defacement. But that is not my affair. I am content with the present moment. I think of nothing beyond that, and I endure the work of this gifted master without understanding it or troubling myself about it."

Yes! Give to God what belongs to him and remain lovingly pliable in his hands. Hold for certain that what takes place, either outwardly or within you, is best for you.

Allow God to act, and give yourself completely to him. Let the chisel perform its task, the sharp needle do its work. Let the artist's brush cover the canvas with many tints that only appear to smear your canvas. Cooperate with all these divine operations by a wholehearted, steady submission, forgetting yourself and enthusiastically giving yourself to duty. Continue in this way in your own allotted path without trying to know all your surroundings or the particular details of the landscape. Proceed on this path without being able to see ahead of you, and you will be shown step by step how to go. Strive first for the kingdom of God and his righteousness by love and obedience, and all the rest will be given to you as well.

We see many people who are distressed about themselves and ask anxiously, "Who will direct us so that we may become humble and holy, and attain perfection?" Let them search in books for the descriptions they find and the characteristics and nature of this marvelous work. But as for you, remain peacefully united to God by love, and follow the clear straight path of duty without looking ahead. The angels are beside you during this time of darkness, and they will bear you up. If God asks more of you, he will make it known to you by his inspirations.

CHAPTER 7

Not Knowing Where the Road Will Lead

When God makes himself the guide of our souls, he requires from us an absolute trust in him and the giving up of any sort of anxious thought about the way he is leading us. We are urged on without being able to see a beaten path before us. We cannot imitate either what we have seen or what we have read, but we must go forward by our own action. We could not do otherwise without a grave risk.

God's action is forever new. It never retraces its steps, but always marks out new paths. Those who are led in this way never know where they are going. Their roads are to be found neither in books nor in their own minds. God's action moves them step by step, and they go forward only by his leading.

When you are conducted by a guide who takes you through an unknown country at night across fields where there are no tracks, by his own skill, asking no advice from anyone, giving no inkling of his plans, what choice do you have but to give yourself completely to his guidance? What use is it to you to find out where you are, to ask passers-by, to consult maps or other travelers? The plans or fancies of a guide who insists on being trusted will have none of this! He will take pleasure in overcoming your anxiety and distrust and will insist that you surrender entirely to his guidance. If you are convinced that he is a good guide, you must have faith in him and abandon yourself to his care.

What God does is essentially good. It does not need to be reformed or controlled. It began at the creation of the world, and his action has manifested ever-fresh energy right up to the present. His operations are limitless, and the possibilities they offer are inexhaustible. He worked in one way yesterday, and today, he works differently. Yet it is the same work applied at each new moment to produce ever-new results, and it will extend from eternity to eternity. This divine action produced Abel, Noah, Abraham—all different. Isaac is an original, as is Jacob. And Joseph is not a copy of either of them. Moses has no prototype among his ancestors. David and the prophets are quite different from the patriarchs. St. John the Baptist stands above them all. Jesus Christ is the First-born. The apostles act more by the guidance of his Spirit than in imitation of his works.

Jesus Christ did not set a limit for his actions, and he did not make his own words into a new legalism. The Holy Spirit ever inspired his holy soul, and since he was completely given to every breath of the Spirit, he had no need to consult the previous moment in order to act in the one that was arriving. The breath of grace shaped every moment according to the eternal pattern of life originating in the invisible and unsearchable wisdom of the Blessed Trinity. The heart of Jesus Christ received these divine directions at every moment and put them into action. The Gospels show a succession of these actions in his life, and this same Jesus who ever lives and works, continues to live and work new things in the souls of his saints.

If you would live according to the Gospels, give yourself completely and simply to the action of God. Jesus Christ is its supreme expression. He "is the same yesterday and today and forever" (Hebrews 13:8). His life continues—it does not need to start over. What he has done is finished. What remains to be done is being carried on in us at every moment. Each saint receives a share in this divine life, and in each, Jesus Christ is different, although the same in himself. The life of each saint is the life of Jesus Christ; it is a new gospel. The cheeks of the Bride are compared to a bed of flowers, to gardens filled with fragrant blossoms. God in us is the gardener, beautifully arranging the flowerbeds. Any particular garden resembles no other, for among all the flowers, no two are alike. No two may even be described as being the same, except in the faithfulness with which they respond to the action of the Creator, in leaving him free to do what he wills, and for their part, obeying the laws that their natures require. Let God act, and let us do what he requires of us: this is the gospel. This is the whole of Scripture. This is the law for everyone.

CHAPTER 8
A Simple, Wonderful Secret

Such, then, is the straight path to saintliness. Such is the state of perfection and such are the duties it imposes on us. And such is the great and incomparable secret of self-surrender, a secret that is, in reality, no secret at all, an art without art.

God, who requires it of everyone, has explained it clearly and made it quite simple and easily understood. The obscurity of the way of pure faith is in nothing that we have to do ourselves. In fact, there is nothing easier to understand or clearer. The only mystery lies in what is done by God.

This is exactly what takes place in the Blessed Eucharist. What is necessary to transform bread into the Body of Jesus Christ is so clear and easy that the most ignorant priest is capable of doing it. Yet it is the mystery of mysteries, where everything is so hidden, so shadowy, so incomprehensible, that the more spiritual and enlightened one becomes, the more faith is required to believe it.

The road of pure faith presents something quite similar. Its effect is to enable us to find God at each moment. It is this that makes it so exalted, so heavenly, so blessed. It is an inexhaustible resource of thought, preaching, and writing. It is a whole collection of—in fact, it is the source of—wonders. To produce such wondrous effects, only one thing is necessary: to let God act and do all that he wills, according to our state in life. Nothing in the spiritual life could be easier, nothing more within the grasp of everyone. And yet, nothing could be more full of wonders, no path more full of shadows. To walk in it, we have need of great faith—all the more so because our reasoning is always so full of suspicions and always ready to make some argument against this way. The soul's ideas are confused by it, for there is nothing in it that reason has ever known or read about, or been used to admiring. It is something entirely new. "The prophets were saints, but this Jesus is a sorcerer," said the unbelieving Jews. If our souls, following their example, are scandalized, we show very little faith, and we well deserve to be deprived of those wonderful things that God is so ready to work in the hearts of the faithful.

BOOK IV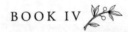

TRIALS CONNECTED WITH THE STATE OF FULL SURRENDER

CHAPTER 1

The First Trial: Unwise Counsel

There is no spiritual path more secure than that of giving yourself entirely to God, no way more easy, sweet, clear, and less subject to illusion and error. In this way, God is loved and all Christian duties are fulfilled. The sacraments are frequented and all the external acts of religion that are binding to everyone are performed. Superiors are obeyed and the duties of one's state of life are fulfilled. Temptations of the flesh, the world, and the devil are continually resisted, for none are more on guard or more vigilant in fulfilling their obligations than those who follow this way.

If this is the case, why should those who follow it be subject to so many assaults from others? The most usual of these is that when they, like other Christians, have accomplished all that the most strict theologian could ask, they are expected also to be bound to certain inconvenient practices that the Church in no way places on them as obligatory. If they do not comply with these, some people charge them with laboring under illusion.

But let us take "nominal" Christians who confine themselves to observing God's commandments and those of the Church, and who besides doing this attend to their worldly business and other affairs of their lives without practicing meditation, contemplation, or spiritual reading, and without being attached to any particular form of devotional life. I ask, are they wrong? We would not think of accusing or even of suspecting them of error! Admitting this to ourselves, and leaving such Christians in peace, it is only fair not to trouble those who not only fulfill the precepts at least as well as the Christians I have just mentioned, but who in addition practice other acts of piety that are either unknown to nominal Christians, or if known, are ignored.

Prejudice goes so far as to affirm that these people are deceiving themselves and are deluded, because, having submitted to all the Church subscribes, they hold themselves free to give themselves without hindrance to the interior movements of God in their hearts and to heed the impressions he makes there when there is no express requirement to do so. In a word, these persons are condemned because they use the time that others give over to amusements and worldly affairs, in loving God. Is not this a crying injustice? We cannot insist on this point too strongly! If anyone keeps the ordinary course and goes to confession once a year, nothing is said about it. That person is left in peace with only an occasional exhortation to do something more, but is not pressed too strongly about it, and is not actually required to do any more. But, if we decide to change our ways and want to improve them, we are overwhelmed with counsels concerning how to live, and given all sorts of different methods. And if we do not follow these pious rules diligently, then we are condemned! We are objects of suspicion, and people predict the very worst concerning us.

Are they not aware that these practices they suggest, however good and holy they may be, are after all, only the way that leads to union with God? Is it necessary, then, to be always on the road when one has already arrived at the goal?

Yet this is exactly what is demanded of those who are supposed to be laboring under illusion. These people have made their way like others at the beginning. Like all the others, they know what to do and have done it faithfully. It would be useless now to try to keep them bound to the same practices. Since God, moved by the efforts they have made to go forward with these various helps, has taken it on himself to lead them to this happy union with himself, they have begun to possess God through love from the very moment they arrived at this blessed state of full surrender. In short, from the time that the God of all goodness relieved these souls of all their struggle and effort and made himself the moving force of all their actions, those first methods lost all their value and became only the road over which such souls had once traveled. To insist that these methods must be resumed and constantly followed would be to make these people abandon the very end and goal at which they had arrived, to reenter the path that led to it!

But if they have any experience, the time and trouble of those who counsel them in this way is wasted. They pursue their noisy, insistent expressions in vain. The surrendered souls will turn a deaf ear to them, and remain untroubled and unmoved in that intimate peace in which they so intimately exercise their love. That is the center in which they will rest, or, if you prefer, that is the straight line marked out by the hand of God. The faithful will continue to walk along this line because all their duties are plainly marked out on it, and by following it they fulfill these duties as they come up, without confusion or haste. As for all the rest, they hold themselves in perfect freedom, always ready to obey every movement of grace immediately when they perceive it, and they give themselves wholly into the care of Providence.

God makes known to these souls that he intends to be their Master and direct them by his grace. He makes them understand that they cannot allow their own freedom to be fettered without denying the sovereign rights of their Creator. They sense that if they were to tie themselves down to the rules of those who live by their own efforts and industry, instead of obeying the leadings of grace, they would deprive themselves of many things they will need to be able to fulfill future duties. But, since no one knows this, they are judged and condemned for their simplicity. They, who find no fault with others, but approve of every state and know well how to discern every degree of progress, are despised by those who pretend to be wise, who cannot appreciate this sweet and hearty submission to divine Providence.

Worldly wisdom cannot understand the perpetual wanderings of the apostles, who did not settle anywhere. Ordinary spirituality cannot tolerate the idea that persons should depend on divine Providence to guide all their actions. There are very few of those in this ordinary state who approve of these self-surrendered souls. But God, who teaches us by means of our fellow creatures, always brings such souls into contact with those who have given themselves to him with single-heartedness and fidelity.

These submitted souls have arrived where they are with the help of good directors, and consequently need less human aid than others. If they find they are occasionally left to themselves, it is because God's Providence has removed, by death or by some other circumstance, those who have guided them in this. Even then, they are always willing to be guided, and only await in peace the moment Providence has arranged.

During the time when they have no director, from time to time they will meet someone in whom they feel they can confide as God leads them, although they may be complete strangers. This is a sign that he makes use of such strangers to clarify certain points, even if the contact is merely temporary. They ask advice, and when it is given, they follow it with the greatest willingness.

But if such help does not appear, they go back to the fundamentals given by their first directors. In this way they are always very well directed, either by the old principles formerly received, or by the counsel of these other directors they encounter, and they make use of everything until God sends them another person or persons in whom they can confide and who will show them his will.

CHAPTER 2

The Second Trial: Unjust Judgments of Others

The second trial of souls who are led by God in this way is the result of their apparent uselessness and their visible defects. There is no honor or reward in service that is concealed, often enough, under the most utter incapacity and uselessness as far as the world is concerned. Doubtless those who are given far more important positions are not, on this account, necessarily excluded from this state of full surrender, and less still is this state incompatible with outstanding virtue and the saintliness that attracts universal veneration.

All the same, there are a far greater number of souls brought to this sublime state whose virtue is known only to God. Such people are little suited for worldly business or affairs, for complicated concerns, or for putting their minds into industrious activities. They seem quite useless. There is nothing noticeable in them but weakness of the body, the mind, the imagination, and the emotions. They take no notice of anything. They are, so to speak, quite stupid, and possess nothing of that culture, study, or reflection that go to the making of a person. Their natures are more like those of children who have not yet been schooled. They have noticeable faults that, without making them any guiltier than children, still cause greater offense. God takes away everything but their innocence, so that they should have nothing to rely on but him alone.

The world, failing to understand this mystery, can judge only by appearance. It can find nothing in them to its taste, nothing that it deems valuable. And so it rejects and despises them, and they are consequently exposed to censure from everyone. The more closely they are observed, the less they are thought of, and the greater the opposition they encounter. Some hidden voice seems to speak in their favor, yet people prefer to listen to their own malicious presuppositions rather than follow this instinct, or at least suspend their judgment of them. People pry into their actions to find out their opinions, and, like the Pharisees who could not endure the actions of Jesus, people regard them with such prejudice that everything they do appears either ridiculous or even criminal.

CHAPTER 3

The Third Trial: Interior Humiliations

Insignificant as they are in the eyes of others, those who are led by God to this state of complete surrender are far more contemptible in their own eyes. There is nothing in what they do or in what they suffer that is not altogether worthless and humiliating. There is nothing striking in anything about them: everything is commonplace. Interiorly there is nothing but trouble and affliction, and exteriorly they meet only contradictions and disappointments. They are feeble in body, requiring many helps and comforts that would seem to be the very opposite of the life of austerity and poverty so admired in the saints. These souls undertake neither heroic deeds, nor fasts, nor great almsgiving, nor ardent, far-reaching zeal.

United to God by faith and love, they see nothing but disorder in themselves. They despise themselves even more when they compare themselves with others who pass for saints, not only adapting themselves to rules and spiritual methods with great ease, but also displaying only what is considered normal and praiseworthy. Therefore their own shortcomings in this respect fill them with confusion and are unbearable to them. This is why they give way to sighs and bitter tears, expressing the grief with which they are oppressed. Let us remember that Jesus Christ was both God and human. As a human he was destroyed, and as God he remained full of glory. These souls share in the sadness and misery of his sufferings, but have no participation in his glory. People regard them in the same way as Herod and his court regarded Jesus.

These poor souls, therefore, are nourished, as far as their senses and minds are concerned, with a most abhorrent food in which they can find no pleasure. They aspire to something quite different, but all the avenues that lead to the saintliness they so much desire remain closed to them. They must live on this bread of suffering, on this bread mingled with ashes, with a continual diminishment, interior and exterior. They have formed an idea of saintliness that gives them constant torments that cannot be relieved. Their will hungers for it, but is powerless to practice it. Why should this be, except to mortify the soul in its most spiritual and intimate part, so that finding no satisfaction or pleasure in anything that happens to it, it must place all its affection in God, who is leading it expressly by this way to make it find pleasure in him alone?

It seems to me that it is easy to conclude from all this that those who have given themselves completely to God in this way cannot occupy themselves, as others do, with desires, examinations, cares, or attachment to certain persons. Neither can they form plans or lay down methodical rules for action or for reading. This would mean that they still have power to dispose themselves, and it would exclude entirely this state of self-emptying to which they are called. In this state they give up to God all their rights over themselves, over their words, actions, thoughts, and plans, and over the way they use their time and everything connected with it. There remains with them only one desire: to keep their eyes fixed on the Master they have chosen, and to listen to the expression of his will in order to carry it out immediately. No condition can better represent this state than that of servants who obey every order they receive, and do not spend their time attending to their own affairs. They neglect these in order to serve their Master at every moment.

Such souls, then, should not be distressed at their impotence. They are able to do much in being able to give themselves completely to a Master who is all-powerful and able to work wonders with the feeblest of instruments if they offer no resistance.

Let us then endure the external conditions of our lives that result in humiliations in our own eyes and in the eyes of others. Rather, let us hide ourselves behind these outward appearances and enjoy God, who is the sole source of all that is good in us. Let us profit by our failures, by our necessities in the matter of food and comfort, by the contempt of others, by our fears, uncertainties, troubles, and all the rest, so as to find all our happiness in God, who by these very means gives himself entirely to us as our only good.

God wishes to dwell within us in our poverty, without all those attributes of saintliness that bring admiration to others, and this is because God would have himself to be the sole nourishment for our souls and the only object of our desires. We are so weak that if we displayed the greater virtues of zeal, liberality, poverty, and austerity, we would make them objects of joy. But as it is, everything is disagreeable in order that God himself may be our whole means of making us holy, our whole support, so that the world despises us and forsakes us to enjoy our treasure in peace. God wishes to be the foundation, the origin of all that is holy in us, and therefore what depends on us and our active faithfulness is very small indeed, and appears quite the opposite of holiness.

There cannot be anything great in us in the sight of God except our willingness to endure. Therefore, let us think of it no more. Let us leave the care of it to God, who knows very well how to bring it about. It all depends on the watchful care and the particular work of divine Providence, and is accomplished for the most part without our knowledge, even in ways that are unexpected and disagreeable to us.

Let us fulfill the little duties of our active faithfulness peacefully, without wanting those that are greater, because God does not wish to give himself to us through our own efforts. We will become saints of God by his grace, and by his special Providence. He knows what rank to give us, so let us leave it to him without forming false ideas or vain systems of holiness for ourselves. Let us continue loving him without ceasing, pursuing with single-heartedness the path he has marked out for us, where everything in us is so poor and paltry in our own eyes and in the eyes of the world.

CHAPTER 4

The Fourth Trial: Distrust of Self

For those who desire nothing else but the will of God, what could be more miserable than not to be able to be sure that they love him? In other days, their minds were enlightened to perceive the plan of perfection, but they are no longer able to see it in their present state. Perfection is being given to them in a way contrary to all preconceived ideas, to all previous enlightenment, to all feeling. It is given by all the crosses sent by Providence, by the work of present duties, and by certain leadings that have nothing good in them except that they do not lead into sin. But all this seems far from the dazzling sublimity of holiness and all that is unusual in virtue.

God and his grace are given in a hidden and strange way, for these souls feel too weak to bear the weight of their crosses, and are disgusted with their obligations. Their attractions are only for quite ordinary devotional exercises. The ideal they have formed of saintliness inwardly rebukes them for their poor and contemptible dispositions. All the books telling of the lives of saints condemn them, for they can find nothing in them to vindicate their own conduct. In them they see the brilliance of holiness, and it makes them downcast because they do not have the strength to attain to it. They do not see that their very weakness is divinely ordered, but look on it as laxity.

All the people they know who are noted for their striking spirituality and sublime contemplations simply despise them. "What a strange saint," they say. And these souls, believing this, are overwhelmed by countless useless efforts to raise themselves up from their low condition. They are heaped with disgrace and have nothing to put forward in their own favor, either to themselves or others.

In this state, these souls feel that they are lost. The reflections that once guided them no longer afford any help. Grace seems to have failed them. Yet it is through this very loss that they find that same grace again, coming in a different form and restoring a hundred times more than it took away, by the purity of its inward impressions.

Without any doubt, this is a deathblow to the soul, for it loses sight of God's will, which, in a manner of speaking, withdraws from before it, to stand behind the soul and push it on. In this way God's will becomes our invisible moving force rather than our clearly perceived object.

Experience proves that nothing kindles the desire for God's will more keenly than this apparent loss. Therefore, the soul vehemently desires to be made one with God's will, and gives vent to the deepest groans—yet finds no consolation anywhere.

A heart that has no other wish but to possess God must attract God to itself, and this secret of love is a very great one, since by this way alone sure faith and firm hope are established in the soul. Then it is that we believe what we cannot see and expect to possess what we cannot feel. How we are perfected by this incomprehensible action, of which we are both the recipient and the instrument without even realizing it!

Everything we do seems to be either by chance or by natural inclination, and is very humbling to the soul. When we are inspired to speak, it seems as if we speak only from ourselves. We never see by what Spirit we are urged to speak. The most divine inspiration frightens us, and whatever we do or feel becomes a source of perpetual self-contempt, as though we were completely faulty and imperfect. We always admire others, and we feel very inferior to them, while their whole way of acting causes us confusion. We distrust our own judgments and cannot be certain about any of our thoughts. We pay excessive submission to the least advice given by a respectable authority, and God's will, keeping us from having any impressive virtue, seems to plunge us into deeper humility. But it does not seem like humility to the soul. As we view it, we are simply getting what we deserve.

The most amazing thing about this is, that in the eyes of others who are not enlightened by God, we appear to be moved by feelings absolutely contrary to virtue: pure obstinacy, disobedience, troublesomeness, contempt, and indignation, for which there seems to be no remedy. The more earnestly we try to overcome these faults, the more they increase, because they form part of the design of God as being the most suitable way of detaching us from the self-life, to prepare us for union with him.

It is from this sad trial that the primary merit of this state of surrender comes. In this trial, everything in nature conspires to draw us back from the narrow path of love and simple obedience, and it requires heroic strength and courage to keep firm in plain, active faithfulness and to sing our part in a song, while grace sings a second part that seems to show by its very notes our lostness and error. All that we can hear is the message of our wrongness, however, and if we have the courage to let the thunder roll, the lightning flash, and the tempest roar, walking with a firm step the path of love, obedience, duty, and the leadings that come moment by moment, the experience can be compared to the soul of Jesus during his suffering, when our divine Savior walked steadfastly in the path of love of his Father and in submission to his will. This path imposed on him tasks that looked quite inconsistent with the dignity of a soul of such holiness as his.

The hearts of Jesus and Mary, bearing the fury of that darkest of nights, let the clouds gather and the storms rage. A multitude of things having every appearance of being opposed to the purpose of God and his will overwhelmed all their senses. But though deprived of all outward support, they walked without faltering in the path of love and obedience. Their eyes were fixed only on what they had to do, and leaving God to act as he pleased with all that concerned them, they endured the whole weight of his divine action. They groaned under the burden, but not for a single moment did they waver or pause. They believed that all would be well, provided they kept on their way and let God act.

CHAPTER 5

The Happy Result of These Trials

In the path of pure faith that has been described, everything that takes place, physically and spiritually, temporarily has the aspect of death. This should not surprise us. What else could we expect? It is natural to this state. God has his own design for each soul, and under the disguise of death carries out those designs very successfully. Under the term "disguise" I refer to all failures, bodily afflictions, and spiritual weakness. All of these succeed and are turned to good in the hands of God. It is by these very things that are a trouble to nature that he prepares to accomplish his highest designs. "All things work together for good for those who love God, who are called according to his purpose" (Romans 8:28). He brings life out of the shadow of death. Therefore, when nature is afraid, faith, taking all for the best, is full of courage and confidence.

Since we know that God's operation encompasses, leads, and accomplishes all things except sin, it is the duty of faith to worship and love it in all things, and to receive it with open arms. We must give ourselves to it with joy and confidence in everything, rising above the appearances that by their very obscurity cause faith to be victorious. This is the way to honor God and to acknowledge him to be God.

To live by faith is to live by joy, confidence, and certainty about all that has to be done or suffered at each moment by God's will. It is in order to give spirit and support to this life of faith and to maintain it that God allows us to be plunged into and carried away by the rough waters of numerous pains, troubles, difficulties, weaknesses, and defeats. For it requires faith to find God in all these. The divine life is given to us at every moment in a hidden but very sure way, under different appearances—such as the death of the body, the supposed loss of the soul, and loss in earthly affairs. In all these, faith finds its nourishment and strength. It pierces through them all and clings to the hand of God, the Giver of life.

Through everything that does not partake of sin, the faithful soul should go forward with confidence, taking each circumstance as a veil, or a disguise of God. His immediate presence alarms, yet at the same time reassures its senses. In fact, this great God who consoles the humble gives the soul in the midst of its greatest desolation an interior assurance that it has nothing to fear, provided it allows him to act and gives itself entirely to him. Although we are grieved when we have lost the sense of the presence of our Well-beloved, something still assures us that we possess him. We are troubled and disturbed, yet nevertheless in our depths we have some unseen anchor that keeps us clinging to God.

"Surely," said Jacob, "the LORD is in this place—and I did not know it!" (Genesis 28:16). You search for God, yet he is everywhere. Everything proclaims him; everything gives him to you. He walks by your side, is around you and within you: there he dwells, and yet you search for him. What you are really searching for is your own idea of God, while all the time you possess him as he really is! You search for perfection, and it is in everything that comes to you. Your sufferings, your actions, your leadings are the sacramental "elements," so to speak, under which God gives himself to you, while you are vainly striving after sublime ideas. But God will not come to you clothed in them.

Martha tried to please Jesus by cooking nice dishes, but Mary was content to be with Jesus in any way he wished to give himself to her. However, when Mary sought him outside the garden tomb according to the idea she had formed of him, he eluded her by presenting himself in the form of a gardener. The apostles saw Jesus, but mistook him for a ghost.

God disguises himself, therefore, to raise the soul to a state of pure faith, to teach it to find him under all kinds of appearances, for when we have discovered this secret of God, he can no longer disguise himself. Faith says, "Look, there he stands, behind our wall, gazing in at the windows, looking through the lattice" (Song of Solomon 2:9).

Divine Love, hide yourself! Proceed from one trial to another, bind my soul by leadings and by duties; blend, confuse, or break like threads all the ideas and methods of my soul. Let me stray here and there for lack of light, and be unable to see or understand in what path I should walk. Formerly I found you dwelling in your ordinary external appearance, in peaceful repose of solitude and prayer, or in suffering. I even found you in the consolations you give to others in the course of conversation or of business. But now, having tried every method I know to please you, I am at a loss, not seeing you in any of these things as in times past. May the fruitlessness of my efforts teach me to search for you from now on in yourself, which means to search for you everywhere, and in all things, without distinction and without reflection.

Divine Love! What a mistake it is not to find you in all that is good and in every created thing. Why then should I search for you in any other way than that by which you desire to give yourself? Why, divine Love, search for you under any other elements than those you have chosen for your sacrament? The less there is to be seen or felt, so much more scope there is for faith and obedience. Do you not give fruitfulness from the root that is hidden underground, and can you not, if you so will, make fruitful this darkness in which you are pleased to keep me?

Live then, little root of my heart, in the deep invisible bosom of God. And by its power, send forth branches, leaves, flowers, and fruit, which, though invisible to yourself, are a joy and nourishment to others. Give of your shade, your flowers, and your fruit to others, unmindful of your own tastes. May all that are grafted on you receive that same life-flow that will be manifested in their own particular growth and appearances. Become all to all, but as far as you yourself are concerned, be completely given and ready to accept whatever comes.

Remain in the dark and confining prison of your wretched cocoon, little worm, until the warmth of grace warms you and causes you to spread your wings. Then feed upon whatever leaves grace offers you and do not regret, in the act of giving yourself to God, any peace you feel you have lost. Stop immediately when God's will bids you stop, and be content to lose all your old formulas, methods, and ways in the alternations between rest and activity, and in the many changes you cannot understand, so as to take upon you what God's will designs for you. In this way you will spin your silk in secret, doing what you cannot see or feel. You will discover in yourself a secret agitation that you yourself will condemn. You envy your companions who seem entirely dead to self, but who have not yet arrived where you are. You continue to admire them, though in truth you have gone on beyond them. May it all work in you to keep you spinning a silk in which the princes of the Church and of the world will happily be clothed.

After that, what will become of you, little worm? By what opening will you emerge from your cocoon? Oh! marvel of grace by which souls are molded in so many different shapes! Who can guess in what direction grace will guide you? In the same way, who could guess what nature does with a silkworm without seeing it working? It is only necessary to provide it with leaves, and nature does the rest.

Therefore, dear souls, no one can tell from where we came or toward where we are going. Neither can we know from what thought of God his wisdom drew us, nor what he intends for us. Nothing is left but to willingly give ourselves to him, and to allow his divine wisdom to act without interfering with it by our own ideas, without choosing our own models or methods. We must act when the time to act comes, and stop when it is time to stop. If necessary, we must let everything be lost, and as a result, according to his leading and our surrender to him, we will act or refrain from action without knowing what the outcome will be. After many changes, the soul formed in this way will receive wings and fly up to heaven, leaving a plentiful harvest on earth for other souls to gather.

BOOK V

GOD'S EVER-PRESENT HELP

CHAPTER 1

Songs in the Night

There is a sort of holiness in which all the communications of God are luminous and distinct. By contrast, on the road of complete yieldedness and faith, everything that God communicates partakes of that inaccessible darkness that surrounds his throne; the ideas that come to the soul are confused and blurred. In this state of obscurity, the soul is often, like the prophet, afraid of running headlong into rocky shoals.

Do not be afraid, faithful soul, for this is your right path; this is the way by which God leads you. There is no more safe and sure way than this unlit path of faith.

"But," you say, "it is so dark that I cannot tell which way to go."

Go wherever you please; you cannot lose the way where there is no path. Every way looks the same in the dark, and you cannot see the end, because nothing is visible.

"But I am afraid of everything. I feel as if I might fall over a cliff at any moment. Everything is an affliction to me. I know very well that I am acting in full surrender of myself to God, but it seems to me that there are things I cannot do without acting contrary to virtue. I seem to be so far from all the virtues. The more I wish to practice them, the more remote they seem. I love virtue, but the dim impressions by which I am led seem to keep virtue far from me. I always give in to this leading, and although I cannot perceive that it guides me well, I cannot help following it. My spirit longs for light, but my heart is in darkness. Enlightened persons and those with clear minds are very pleasing to my spirit, but when I hear them speak or listen to sermons, my heart understands nothing. It is inspired only by the gift of faith, which makes it love and appreciate the source, the truth, the path where it has neither aim nor ideas, even when it trembles, shudders, and falters. I have an assurance, I do not know how, in the depths of my heart, that this way is right—not by any evidence of my senses, but by a feeling inspired by faith."

This is because it is impossible that God should lead a soul without assuring it that the path is a right one, and this with a certainty all the greater the less it seems so. And this certainty is greater than fantasies, fears, struggles, and all imaginations. The mind cries out vainly and searches for some better way. We recognize the Lord unconsciously, but when we reach out to hold him, he disappears. We feel the Lord's protective hand surrounding us, and we prefer to wander in a seemingly aimless way, gently yielding ourselves to his guidance rather than trying to gain some self-confidence by following the beaten paths of virtue.

Let us go to God, then, in complete yieldedness, and let us freely acknowledge that we are incapable of acquiring virtue by our own industry or effort. But let us not allow this absence of particular virtues to diminish our confidence. Our divine Guide would never have reduced us to the necessity of walking this way if he had not intended to carry us in his arms. What need do we have of light and certainty, of ideas and reflections? Of what use would it be to us to see, to know, and to feel, when we are no longer having to walk, but are being carried in the arms of your divine Providence? The more we have to suffer from darkness, the more rocks, cliffs, and deserts there are in our way, the more we have to endure from fears, dry times, weariness of mind, anguish of soul, and even despair—the greater must be our confidence and faith! One glance at him who carries us is sufficient to restore our courage in the greatest peril.

Then we will forget the paths and what they are like. We will even forget ourselves, and giving ourselves with glad abandon to the wisdom, goodness, and power of our Guide, we will think only of loving him. We will avoid all sin—not only that which is evident, but the very appearance of evil as well—and will fulfill all the obligations imposed upon us by our state in life.

This is the only responsibility you lay on your little children, dear Lord! All the rest you take upon yourself. The more terrible "all the rest" may be, the more surely can we feel and recognize your presence. Your children need only to love you without ceasing, and to fulfill their little duties like a child on its mother's lap who is occupied only with its games as if it had nothing else to do but play with its mother. The soul should soar beyond the clouds. Night is not the time for working, but for repose. The light of reason can do nothing but intensify the darkness of faith; the radiance needed to penetrate the darkness must come from on high.

In this state of pure faith, God communicates himself to us as our life, but he is no longer visible as our way and truth. We search for the Lord during the night, eagerly hurrying toward him, only to find that he is behind us, holding us with his hands and guiding us. No longer is he the object of faith, or an idea: he has become the Author and Source of our faith. For all the needs, difficulties, troubles, falls, defeats, persecutions, and uncertainties of those who have lost all confidence in themselves and their own abilities, there are secret and inspired resources in God's action, marvelous and unknown.

The more perplexing the circumstances, the more keenly we anticipate a satisfactory solution. The heart says, "All is going well. It is God who is carrying on this work. There is nothing to fear." That very fear, that suspense and distress are verses of the songs in the night. It is a joy that not a single syllable is omitted, and it all ends in a *Gloria Patri*.[2] As we go on our way of wanderings, darkness itself serves to guide us and doubts serve to reassure us. The more puzzled Isaac was to find something to offer as a sacrifice, the more completely did Abraham place everything in the hands of Providence, trusting it all to God.

CHAPTER 2

Joy in the Morning

Those who walk in light sing songs of the light. Those who walk in darkness sing the songs of the night. Both must be allowed to sing to the end the part given to them by God in the great Oratorio. Nothing must be added to the score, nothing left out. Every drop of bitterness must be allowed to flow freely, no matter what it costs. It was so with Jeremiah and Ezekiel, whose utterances were broken by tears and sobs, who could find no consolation except in continuing their lamentations. Had the course of their grief been interrupted, we would have lost the most beautiful passages of Holy Scripture. The Spirit that afflicts is the only one that can console. These diverse waters flow from the same source. When God appears wrathful, the soul trembles. When he threatens, we are terrified. His divine operation must be allowed to develop, for with the ill it carries a cure.

So continue to weep and tremble! Let restlessness and agony invade your souls. Make no effort to free yourself from these divine terrors, these heavenly troubles, but open your hearts to receive these little streams from that immense sea of sorrows that God bore in his most holy soul. Sow in sorrow for as long as grace brings tears to your eyes, and that same grace will eventually dry your tears. The clouds will disappear before the radiance of the sun. Spring will come with its flowers, and the results of your surrender will be to see the wonderful variety and full extent of God's divine action.

It is truly quite useless for people to trouble themselves. Everything that happens to them is like a dream. One shadowy image follows another, like imaginations drifting through the mind—some sorrowful, some full of consolation. The soul is the playground for these fantasies that devour each other in great rapidity, and as upon awakening from dreams, when they are past, we find that nothing about them could stop the progress of the soul. Awakening dissipates all their remembrance, and we take no notice either of their sorrows or joys.

Lord, it can be truly said that you cradle your children who are asleep in your arms during this long night of faith, and that you are pleased to allow an infinite variety of thoughts to pass through their minds—thoughts that are holy and full of mystery. In the state in which these dreams of the night place them, they do indeed experience terrible torments of fear, anguish, and weariness, but on the bright day of glory, you will make these things disappear and turn into joy.

At the moment of awakening and immediately afterward, these holy souls, now fully restored to themselves and with complete freedom of judgment, will never tire of wondering at the skill, the tact, the loving inventions that their Lord has used. They will understand how unsearchable are his ways, how impossible it is to guess his riddles, to find out his disguises, or to receive consolation when his will brings terror and alarm. At this great awakening, those who, like Jeremiah and David, have been inconsolable in their grief will see that their distress and desolation was a subject of great joy for God and his angels.

Do not awaken these souls with the noise of the world, the bustle of efforts, or of human actions, in spite of the sneers of the skeptics. In their sleep, they sigh and tremble. In their dreams they pursue and search for their Lord who hides himself.

Let them dream. Their fears come only from the night and from their sleep. When their Lord has brought forth in them what only he can express, he will reveal the rest of the dream and waken them at the right time.

Joseph caused Benjamin to weep, and his servants kept his secret from this beloved brother. Joseph deceived him, and not all his wit could fathom this deception. Benjamin and his brothers were plunged into unspeakable sorrow. Joseph was only playing a trick on them, but the poor brothers could see nothing but an evil with no remedy. When Joseph revealed to them who he was and put everything right, they saw his wisdom in making them think that all was lost and in making them despair before revealing the truth, which brought them the greatest joy they had ever experienced.

CHAPTER 3
God's Loving Deceptions

Let us go on further in understanding God's action and its loving deceptions. What he seems to take away from us, he bestows without revealing his identity, so to speak, on those with goodwill. He never allows us to lack anything. It is as if someone who had been sustained by the generosity that a friend had bestowed personally on him, should suddenly, for his own good, have such a friend pretend suddenly that he could no longer help him, and yet should continue to assist him anonymously. The friend, not suspecting any stratagem in this mystery of love, would feel hurt, and might well entertain all kinds of ideas and criticisms about the conduct of his benefactor.

When, however, the mystery begins to be unveiled, God knows what feelings arise in the soul: joy, tenderness, gratitude, love, admiration, and shame for its accusations. And these are followed by an increase of zeal for and attachment to the benefactor. This sort of trial is the means of strengthening the soul and preparing it for similar surprises.

The application is easy. With God, the more we seem to lose, the more we gain. The more he takes away what is natural, the more he gives of what is supernatural. He is loved at first for his gifts, but when these are no longer perceptible, he is at last loved for himself. It is by the apparent withdrawal of these tangible gifts that he prepares the way for the great gift that is the greatest and most precious of all, since it embraces all other gifts.

Those who have once for all submitted themselves to having God's will prevail in them ought to interpret everything in a favorable light. Yes, everything! Even the loss of excellent spiritual guides and the lack of confidence they cannot help feeling for those who offer to take over that responsibility!

In truth, these guides who, of their own accord, run after souls, deserve to be distrusted. Those who are truly led by the Spirit of God do not, as a rule, show so much eagerness and self-assurance. They do not come forward until they are appealed to, and even then they proceed with caution.

Let those who have given themselves entirely to God pass through all these trials without fear and without losing their freedom. If only they remain faithful to the movement of God within, this all-powerful action can produce marvels in them in spite of everything. God and the soul work together, and the success of the work depends entirely on the divine Workman, and can be spoiled only if we prove unfaithful.

When the soul is well, all is well, because what comes from God, that is to say, his judgment and his action, corresponds exactly to the soul's faithfulness. It is the beautiful side of the work, which is done something like a superb tapestry, stitch by stitch, from the wrong side. The worker employed on it sees only the stitch that is made and the needle that makes it, while all the stitches combined form magnificent figures that do not show until every part is complete and the right side is turned outward. All its beauty and perfection remain in obscurity during its progress.

So it is with the soul that has given itself completely to God. It has eyes only for God and for its duty. Doing this duty at each passing moment is like an imperceptible stitch added to the work, and yet with these stitches God performs wonders of which he sometimes allows us a glimpse, but which will not be entirely visible until the great day of eternity.

How full of goodness and wisdom is God's guidance! He has so entirely retained for his own grace and action all that is admirable, great, exalted, and sublime, and so completely left us, with the aid of grace, all that is little, light, and easy, that there is no one in all the world who cannot easily reach the very pinnacle of holiness by performing with love the most ordinary and common duties.

CHAPTER 4

Grace Through the Ordinary Things

It is particularly in souls wholly given to God that the words of St. John are fulfilled: *[Y]ou do not need anyone to teach you. But . . . his anointing teaches you about all things* (1 John 2:27). To know what God asks of them, they have only to consult their own hearts and listen to the inspirations of this anointing. The heart interprets the will of God according to their present needs.

The divine action, concealed though it is, shows its designs, not through ideas, but intuitively. It shows them to the soul, either by necessity, leaving it no course but the present one to choose; or by a sudden impulse, a sort of supernatural feeling that impels the soul to act without any premeditation; or, finally, by giving it a certain inclination or repulsion, while leaving it completely free, yet none the less leading it to take or refuse what is being presented to it.

If we were to judge by appearances, it would seem as if these souls showed a great lack of virtue, to allow themselves to be moved or swayed in this manner. And if we were to judge by ordinary rules, there would appear to be a lack of discipline and method in such conduct. In reality, however, it is the highest degree of virtue, and only after practicing it a long time can we succeed at it. The virtue of this state is pure virtue. It is, in fact, perfection itself. These souls are like musicians who combine perfect knowledge of music with technical skill. They are then so full of their art that, without thinking, all that they perform is perfect. And if their compositions were examined afterward, they would be seen to be in complete conformity with prescribed rules. We would be convinced then, that they could never succeed better than when they allowed themselves to be free from rules that keep genius in fetters when followed too scrupulously, and their impromptu compositions would be admired by connoisseurs like so many masterpieces.

In the same way, the soul, trained for a long time in the study and practices of perfection under the sway of human reason and human methods that it uses as an aid to grace, forms within itself a habit of acting by divine instinct in all things. In time, then, such persons seem to know that they can do no better than to do the first duty that presents itself, without resorting to the reasoning they formerly found necessary.

They have only to act without any seeming order or direction when they can trust in nothing but the workings of grace, knowing this cannot mislead them. The effect of grace in such people is nothing short of marvelous to those who have eyes to see it: without rules, yet most exact; without methods, yet most orderly; without premeditation, yet most profound; without skill, yet nothing better proportioned; without effort, yet everything accomplished; without foresight, yet nothing better suited to unexpected events.

Spiritual reading is made by the action of the Spirit to contain meanings the author never thought of. God makes use of the words and actions of others to impart hidden truths. If he wills to enlighten us by such means, we should avail ourselves of this light. Everything that becomes an instrument of his divine action has a value far surpassing its natural and apparent worth.

It is characteristic of this state of yieldedness to God that we are led to a life of mystery—a life that excites wonder and surprise while baffling efforts to comprehend it. It is a life that receives great and miraculous gifts from God by means of the most ordinary and common things, such as happy coincidences or chance encounters, where nothing is apparent to human eyes but the ordinary workings of people's minds and the natural course of the elements. In this way the simplest sermons, the most commonplace conversations, and the least elevating books become to us, by virtue of God's will, sources of wisdom and knowledge. This is why we carefully gather up the crumbs that skeptics trample under foot. Everything is precious in our eyes, everything enriches us, so that while we are deliberately neutral in regard to all things, we do not neglect or despise anything, and make use of them all.

When we see God in all things and use everything by his will, it is not using creatures, but enjoying his divine purpose that is transmitted to us through varying channels. These channels in themselves do not make us holy, but they are only instruments of his divine action. They can be used by God to bring his grace, and they indeed often do communicate his grace to the simple soul in ways and by means that seem the exact contrary to the end proposed. In God's hands, mud is as clear as glass, and the instrument that his grace uses always achieves its purpose. Everything is equally useable as far as grace is concerned. Faith never feels any need. It does not complain of the lack of means that may seem necessary for its advancement, because the divine Workman, who uses all means effectively, supplies by his own action whatever may be lacking. His holy will in action is our entire virtue.

CHAPTER 5
Our Safety in the Hand of God

God's will infallibly directs submissive souls to the right course of action, and these souls respond to his direction within. They are pleased with everything that has taken place, with everything that is happening, and with everything that affects them, with the exception of sin. Sometimes they act, fully conscious of what they are doing. At other times they act unconsciously, moved by obscure leadings to say or do certain things, or to leave other things unsaid or undone, without being able to give reasons for their action.

Often the circumstance and the reason determining it are purely of the natural order of things. Seeing no mystery in it, these souls act by seeming chance, necessity, or convenience, and their acts appear only natural, both to them and to others. All the time, however, God's purpose is being worked out through the intellect, the wisdom, or the counsel of friends, making use of the simplest things in favor of these yielded souls. His grace makes all these things its own, and so persistently opposes every effort that would defeat his purpose, that such efforts are of no avail.

To deal with such a simple, yielded soul is, in a certain sense, to deal with God. What can be done against the will of the Almighty and his designs, which cannot be readily interpreted or understood? God takes the cause of these simple souls in hand. They do not need to worry about the intrigues of others, meeting their activities with equal alertness, watching all their movements. Their Lord relieves them of all these anxieties, and they can rest their hearts in him, peaceful and secure.

God's operation within frees and exempts them from those anxious and low ways that are so necessary to human prudence. Those ways were suitable to Herod and the Pharisees, but the Magi had only to follow their star in peace. The Child had only to rest in his mother's arms. His enemies do more to advance his interests than to hinder his work. The more they try to thwart him and take him unawares, the more freely and tranquilly he acts. He never makes allowances for them or flatters them to escape their blows. Their jealousies, suspicions, and persecutions are necessary to him.

This is the way Jesus Christ lived in Judea, and this is the way he lives now in simple souls. He lives in their hearts, generous, sweet, free, peaceful, fearless, needing no one, seeing all creatures as in his Father's hands and obliged to serve him—some by criminal passions, others by holy actions; the first by their contradictions, the latter by their obedience and submission. God's overarching purpose balances all this in a wonderful manner. Nothing is lacking, nothing is excessive, but of good and evil there is only what is needed.

The will of God brings to every moment the proper means to reach the desired end, and simple souls, taught by faith, find everything to be right, desiring neither more nor less than what they have. They ever bless that divine hand that so well apportions the means needed and turns aside every obstacle in its path. They receive friends and enemies with the same patient courtesy with which Jesus treated everyone, knowing they are instruments in God's purpose. They need no one, yet they need everyone. God's purpose makes all of them necessary, and they must be received according to their quality and nature, and responded to with sweetness and humility—that is to say, the simple are to be treated simply, and the uncouth with kindness. This is what St. Paul taught and what Jesus Christ practiced most perfectly.

Only grace can impress this supernatural character in us, enabling us to adapt ourselves to what is appropriate to each person. This is never learned from books, but from a true spirit of prophecy. It is the result of special inspiration and teaching from the Holy Spirit. To understand it, we must be in the highest state of surrender, the most perfectly free from all self-originating designs, and from all personal interests, however holy. We must have in view the only serious business in the world, that of obeying submissively the will of God at work in us. To do this, we must apply ourselves to fulfill the obligations of our station in life, and allow the Holy Spirit to act within us without trying to understand his operations, even being pleased to be kept ignorant of what they are. Then we are truly safe, for all that happens in the world can work nothing but good for those who are perfectly submitted to God's will.

CHAPTER 6

Useful Enemies

I fear my own actions and those of my friends more than those of my enemies. There is no prudence so great as that which offers no resistance to enemies, and which opposes them only by greater submission to God. This is to run before the wind, and since there is nothing else to be done, to keep quiet and peaceful.

There is nothing more entirely opposed to worldly wisdom than simplicity. It turns aside all schemes without understanding them, without so much as a thought about them. God within makes the soul take such just measures as to turn the tables on those who want to take it by surprise, and surprise them instead! The simple soul profits by all the efforts of its enemies, and is raised by the very things that are done to bring it down. They are just galley slaves who bring the ship into port with hard rowing. All obstacles turn to the good of this simple one, and by allowing its enemies a free hand, it obtains their continual service.

The only thing such a soul has to fear is taking part itself in a work that should be left to God and its enemies, a work that it should only observe in peace, following with simplicity the leadings that come from God. The supernatural prudence of the Holy Spirit, the source of the soul's leadings, always infallibly attains its end, and the results of the enemies' attacks are so precisely applied to the soul, without its knowing it, that all who oppose it must inevitably be destroyed.

CHAPTER 7
No Justifying of Self!

The broad, firm, and solid rock upon which the faithful soul rests, sheltered from tides and storms, is the divine will. This will is ever present with us, veiled under crosses or the most ordinary duties. Behind this veil, God's hand is hidden, sustaining and supporting those who give themselves up entirely to him. From the time that we become firmly established in full surrender, we are protected from those whose tongues chatter against us, for we need not ever say or do anything in self-defense. Since the work is of God, justification must never be sought anywhere else. The effects of God's work and its consequences are justification enough. We have only to allow it to develop. "Day to day pours forth speech" (Psalm 19:2).

When we are no longer guided by premeditation, words must no longer be used in self-defense. Our words can only express our own ideas. Where no ideas are supposed to exist, words cannot be used. Of what use would they be? To give a satisfactory explanation of our conduct? But we cannot explain that of which we know nothing, for it is hidden in the source of our behavior, and we have nothing but an impression that we cannot even describe.

We must, therefore, let the results of our actions justify their origins. All the links of this divine chain remain firm and solid, and the purpose of what causes the action is seen in its results. We are no longer living a life of dreams, imaginations, and multitudes of words. We are no longer occupied with these things, nor are we nourished and sustained in this way. They are no longer of any help, and they afford no support.

We no longer see where we are going, nor can we foresee where we will go in the future. Premeditation no longer gives us courage to endure fatigue or sustain the hardships of the way. All this is swept aside by an inner conviction of utter weakness. The path becomes clear just in front of our feet. We have begun on it and we continue on it without hesitation. Being completely single-hearted and straightforward, we follow the path of God's commandments quietly, relying on God himself, whom we find at every step. And God, whom we seek above all things, takes upon himself to show his presence in such a way as to avenge us of our unjust detractors.

CHAPTER 8
No Self-Guidance!

There is a time when God wills to be the life of our souls and work out our perfection himself in a hidden and secret manner. When this time comes, all our own ideas, enlightenment, efforts, inquiries, and reasoning become sources of illusion. And when, after many sad experiences, we have been taught the uselessness of our self-direction, finding that God has hidden and confused all the issues, we are forced to flee to him to find life. Then, convinced of our utter nothingness, realizing that our self-guidance is a hindrance, we throw ourselves into God's providence and rely only on him. It is then that God becomes the source of our life, not by means of our ideas, illuminations, or reflections (for all this is no longer anything to us but a source of illusion). No, he becomes our life in reality, by his grace, which is always hidden under the strangest appearances.

The divine operation being hidden from us, we receive our strength and substance by many circumstances that we think will be our destruction. There is no cure for this ignorance, and it must be allowed to run its course. For here, in this night of faith, God gives himself to us, and with himself, he gives us all things. We are now just blind subjects, or, in other words, we are like a sick person who knows nothing of the virtue of his medicines, but only their bitterness. He often thinks that they will be the death of him. The exhaustion and crises that follow them seem to bear out his fears. Nevertheless, it is under this appearance of death that his health is restored, and he continues to take the medicine on the word of the physician.

In the same way, souls who are yielded to God do not bother about their infirmities, except as regards obvious illnesses that require care and treatment. The weariness and lack of strength of faithful souls are only illusions and appearances that they must face with courage. God sends them or permits them, in order to give us opportunities to exercise our faith and our self-surrender, which are the true remedies for our maladies. Without paying the least attention to them, we should generously pursue our way, following God's will in action and in suffering, making use of the body without hesitation, as if it were a hired horse that is intended to be driven at our will. This treatment is better than to give way to thinking of our health so much that we do harm to our souls. This strength of spirit does much to maintain a feeble body, and one year of this noble and generous life is worth more than a century of selfish fears and care.

We must try to habitually maintain an air of childlike gentleness and goodwill. What is there to be afraid of in fulfilling God's will? Guided, sustained, and protected by the providence of God, his children should be nothing less than heroic. The terrifying objects we have met on our way are nothing in themselves. They are sent only that life may be adorned with more glorious victories. They entangle us in troubles of every kind, where human prudence can neither see nor imagine any outlet. It is then we feel all our weakness and, finding out our shortcomings, we are put to shame.

At this point, the divine will gloriously shows what it is for souls who wholly trust in it without reserve. It extricates them more marvelously than fiction writers, in the fertility of their imagination, can unravel the intrigues and perils of their imaginary heroes, who always reach a happy ending. With greater skill and even happier endings, God guides the faithful through deadly perils and monsters, even through the fires of hell with their demons and torments. His action raises their souls to the heights of heaven, and makes them the subjects of tales, both real and mystical, that are more beautiful and more extraordinary than any ever invented by vain human imagination.

Go forward then, my soul, through perils and fears, guided and sustained by that mighty invisible hand of divine providence. Go forward without fear, in joy and peace to the end, turning all the incidences of life into occasions of fresh victories. We march under God's banner, to fight and to conquer. "He came out conquering and to conquer" (Revelation 6:2).

Every step we take under his guidance is a victory. The book of sacred history lies open before the Holy Spirit, and it is still being written, nor will its material be finished till the end of the world. This history is none other than an account of the guidance and designs of God on humankind. All we have to do to appear in its pages and to continue its narration is to unite our actions and sufferings with his will.

No! It is not to cause the loss of our souls that we have so much to do and to suffer, but to furnish us material for the sacred history that is being added to day by day.

CHAPTER 9
God's Love, the Source of All Good

While God deprives of everything the souls who give themselves entirely to him, he gives them something in the place of those things. Instead of light, strength, wisdom, and life, he gives them his love. Divine love is like a supernatural instinct in these souls.

Everything in nature has that which is suited to its kind. Each flower has its special beauty, each animal its instinct, and each creature its perfection. And so it is in the different states of grace. Each has its special grace, and this is the recompense for all those who accept with good will the state in which they are placed by the providence of God.

A soul becomes subject to God's action the moment a good will is formed in it, and God's action influences it more or less, according to the degree of surrender. The whole art of surrender is simply that of loving, and divine action is nothing else than the action of divine Love. How can it be that these two loves seeking each other should do otherwise than unite when they meet? How can divine Love refuse anything to a soul whose every desire he inspires? And how can a soul that lives only for him refuse him anything? Love can refuse nothing that love desires, nor desire anything that love refuses.

The divine action considers only the good will of a soul. The capacity or incapacity of the other faculties neither attracts it nor repels it. All that God's love requires is a heart that is good, pure, just, simple, submissive, and respectful, befitting a son or a daughter. It takes possession of such hearts, and of all their faculties, and so arranges everything for their benefit that they find everything a means of making them holy. That which would destroy others would find in them an antidote of good will that would render its poison harmless. Even at the edge of a precipice, the divine action will draw them back. Even if they were allowed to remain there, it would keep them from falling, and if they should fall, it would rescue them. After all, the faults of such souls are only faults of weakness. Love takes but little notice of them and well knows how to turn them to advantage.

By secret suggestions, God makes such souls understand what they ought to say or do, according to the circumstances. They receive these intimations as rays of light from the divine understanding: "all those who practice it have a good understanding" (Psalm 111:10). For this divine intelligence accompanies them in all their wanderings and rescues them from the false steps that their simplicity encourages. Have they committed themselves by some promise that is prejudicial to them? Divine providence arranges some fortunate occurrence that rectifies everything. In vain are intrigues repeatedly formed against them. Divine providence cuts all the knots, brings the enemies to confusion, and so turns their heads as to make them fall into their own trap. Do their enemies try to catch them by surprise? Providence, by means of some apparently unimportant action that the faithful unconsciously do, rescues them from the embarrassments into which they have been led by their own uprightness and the malice of their enemies.

What wisdom it is to have good will! What prudence is there in simplicity! What ingenuity in its innocence and frankness! What mysteries and secrets there are in its straightforwardness!

Look at the youthful Tobit. He was just a young man, yet with what confidence he proceeded, having the archangel Raphael for his guide. Nothing frightened him, and he lacked nothing. The very monsters he encountered furnished him with food and medicines. The one that rushed forward to eat him became itself his food. By the order of Providence, he had nothing to attend to but feasts and weddings, and everything else was left to the guiding spirit appointed to help him. These other affairs were so well managed that they had never before been so successful, blessed, and prosperous. His mother wept, in great distress, believing she had lost him, but his father remained full of faith. The son, so bitterly mourned, returned to become the happiness of his family.

Divine love, then, is the source of all good for those souls who wholly give themselves up to it. To acquire this inestimable blessing the only thing necessary is an earnest desire for it.

Yes, dear souls, God asks only for your heart. If you seek, you will find this treasure, this kingdom where God alone reigns. If your heart is entirely devoted to God, it is itself, for that very reason, the treasure and the kingdom you search for and desire. From the time that we desire God and his holy will, we enjoy God and his will, and our enjoyment corresponds to the intensity of our desire. The earnest desire to love God is truly to love him. Because we love him, we desire to be the instruments of his action so that his love may freely operate in us and through us.

The work of God's divine operation is not measured by the abilities of those who are fully surrendered to him, or by the steps they take, or the means they use, but by the purity of their intention. It is not unusual for them to be deceived in their plans and actions, but their good intention and good will can never deceive them. As long as God sees a good intention in them, he can overlook the rest, and he accepts as done what they would certainly do if truer ideas backed up their good will.

Good will, therefore, has nothing to fear. If it falls, it can only do so under the almighty hand that guides and sustains it in all its wanderings. It is this divine hand that turns it again to face the goal when it has wandered from the path. In that hand the soul finds its resource when it has been deceived by its blind faculties and has been misled. The soul learns to despise these faculties and to rely on God alone, giving itself absolutely to his infallible guidance. Even the errors into which such faithful souls fall lead them into greater surrender to God. Never will good will find itself unaided. That all things work for its good is an article of faith!

CHAPTER 10
Grace to the Humble of Heart

Of what use are the most sublime illuminations, the most divine revelations, if we have no love for the will of God? It was because of this that Lucifer fell. The plan of God's action, revealed to him by God in showing him the mystery of the Incarnation, produced nothing in him but envy.

On the other hand, a simple soul, enlightened only by faith, can never tire of praising, admiring, and loving the order of

God, recognizing it not only in holy creatures, but even in the most irregular confusion and disorder. One grain of pure faith will give more light to a simple soul than Lucifer received by his sublime revelations.

Our faithful devotion to our obligations, our quiet submission to the inner promptings of grace, our gentleness and humility toward everyone, are of more value than the most profound insight into mysteries. If we would learn to see only the will of God in all the pride and cruelty of creatures, we would never treat them with anything but sweetness and respect. Their roughness would never disturb God's order, whatever course it might take. We must only see in it God's overarching action, given and taken, as long as we are faithful in the practice of sweetness and humility. It is best not to concern ourselves about their course of behavior, but to keep steadily on in our own path. In this way, with gentle pressure we will break cedars and overturn great boulders.

Who can resist the force of a meek, humble, faithful soul? These are the only weapons to be taken up if we wish to conquer all our enemies. Jesus Christ has placed them in our hands for our defense: there is nothing to fear if we know how to use them. We must not be cowardly, but entirely free. That is the only disposition becoming to those who are chosen to be God's instruments.

All the works of God are sublime and marvelous. Never can a person's own actions, when they are warring against God, resist God's action in someone who is united to his will by sweetness and humility.

What is Lucifer? A brilliant spirit, more enlightened than all the others, but now in rebellion against God and his will. The mystery of sin is merely the continuation of this rebellion in every possible variety. Lucifer, as much as in him lies, will leave no stone unturned to destroy what God has made and ordered. Wherever he enters, there the work of God is defaced. The more light, knowledge, and ability we have, the greater our danger if we do not possess the foundation of piety that consists in submission to the will of God. It is a disciplined, submissive heart that unites us to God's purposes. Without that, all our goodness is just purely natural, generally in direct opposition to the divine order. God makes use only of the humble as his instruments. Though the proud always resist him, he yet makes use of them, like slaves, for the accomplishment of his designs.

When I find a soul whose first object is God and submission to his will, however lacking it may be in all else, I say, "This is a soul with a great aptitude for serving God." The Blessed Virgin and St. Joseph were like this. Other gifts without this one alarm me. I am afraid of seeing a repetition of Lucifer's actions in them. I remain on my guard, and I entrench myself in my simplicity to resist all this outward glitter of gifts, which, by themselves, are nothing but bits of broken glass.

CHAPTER 11
Simplicity's Strength and Vision

The will of God is the whole life of those who have given themselves to it. They respect this will even in the evil actions of the proud who attempt to abase them. The proud, on the other hand, despise those who see nothing in them. The faithful see only God through the actions of the proud, but the proud mistake their humble manner as a mark of esteem for themselves. Actually, it is only a sign of the loving fear of God and of his holy will that they see in the person of the proud.

No, poor foolish creatures! The submissive souls do not fear you. You excite their compassion. They are answering God when you think they are speaking to you. It is with him that they have to do. They regard you only as one of his slaves, or rather as a shadow that veils him. Therefore, the more overbearing you are, the more humble they become, and when you think you can take them unawares, they surprise you instead. Your tricks intended to deceive them and your violence are just favors from heaven for them.

Proud persons are an enigma to themselves, but the simple soul, with the light of faith, can see very clearly through them.

This recognition of the divine will in all that transpires within us and around us every moment is the true knowledge of things. It is a continual revelation of truth and an unceasingly renewed communication with God. It is the enjoyment of the Lord, not in secret or in stealth, but openly, in public, without fear of any creature. It is a fund of peace, of joy, of love, and of satisfaction with God, whom we see and know, or rather, whom we believe to be living and operating in the most perfect manner in everything that happens. It is the beginning of eternal happiness, though that happiness is still realized and tasted in an incomplete and veiled way.

The Holy Spirit arranges all the pieces on the board of life, and he will, by this fruitful and continual presence of his action, say at the hour of death, "Let there be light!" Then we will see the treasures that faith has hidden in this great space of peace and contentment with God, treasures that were present at every moment of all we did or suffered for him.

When God gives himself in this way, all that is common becomes wonderful. This is the reason nothing seems too extraordinary, because the way itself is extraordinary, and it is unnecessary for it to be full of strange and unsuitable marvels. It is, in itself, a miracle, a revelation, a constant joy even with the prevalence of minor faults. But it is a miracle that, while rendering all common and sensible things wonderful, has nothing in itself that is marvelous to the senses.

CHAPTER 12

Faith's Assurance

If the presence of God's action is hidden here on earth under the appearance of weakness, it is in order to increase the merit of those who are faithful to it. But its triumph is no less certain for that.

The history of the world from the beginning is only the history of the struggle between the powers of the world and of hell against the souls that are humbly submissive to God's action. In the conflict all the advantage seems to be on the side of pride. Yet, the victory always remains with humility.

The world is always represented to our eyes as a statue of gold, brass, iron, and clay. This mystery of iniquity, shown in a dream to Nebuchadnezzar, is nothing but a confused assemblage of all the actions, interior and exterior, of the children of darkness. This is also typified by the beast coming out of the pit to make war from the beginning of time against the interior and spiritual life of mankind. This war still continues in our day. Monster follows monster out of the pit, which swallows and spews them forth again amid incessant clouds of smoke.

The combat between St. Michael and Lucifer that began in heaven continues. The heart of this once magnificent angel has become an inexhaustible, bottomless pit of every kind of evil through his envy. He caused angel to revolt against angel in heaven, and from the creation of the world his whole energy has been exerted to make more criminals among humankind in order to fill the ranks of those who have been swallowed up in the pit. Lucifer is the chief of those who refuse obedience to the Almighty. This mystery of iniquity is the very inversion of God's order. It is the order, or rather, the disorder of the devil.

This disorder is a mystery, because under a false appearance of good, it hides incurable and infinite evil. All wicked persons, who from the time of Cain right up to the present moment have declared war against God, have outwardly been great and powerful, making a great stir in the world and worshiped by all. But this apparent splendor is a mystery. They are just beasts that have ascended from the pit, one after another, to overthrow the order of God. But this order, which is also a mystery, has always opposed them with truly powerful and great persons, who have dealt these monsters a mortal blow. As fast as hell spews them forth, heaven creates fresh heroes to combat them. Ancient history, both sacred and profane, is merely the record of this war. The order of God has ever remained victorious, and those who have ranged themselves on the side of God have shared his triumph and are happy for all eternity. Injustice has never been able to protect deserters from God's cause. Gross wickedness can reward them only by death, eternal death.

Those who practice gross wickedness imagine themselves invincible. But, dearest God, who shall resist you? If all the powers of earth and hell were ranged against one single soul, it need have no fear, if by surrender to you it takes its stand on the side of God and his will.

The monstrous spectacle of wickedness, armed with so much power—the head of gold, the body of silver, brass, and iron—is nothing more than an image of clay. A small stone cast at it will scatter it to the four winds.

How wonderfully the Holy Spirit has illustrated the history of the world. So many startling revelations! So many renowned heroes following each other like so many brilliant stars! So many wonderful events! Yet they are all like the dream of Nebuchadnezzar, forgotten on awaking, however terrible the impression it made at the time.

All these monsters come into the world only to exercise the courage of God's children, and if these children are well trained, God gives them the pleasure of slaying the monsters and continues to send new warriors into the field. This life is a spectacle to angels, causing continual joy in heaven, work for saints on earth, and confusion to the demons in hell.

Therefore, all that is opposed to God's will and order serves only to render it more worthy of being worshiped. The voluntary workers of gross wickedness become the slaves of justice, and from the ruins of Babylon, God's action builds the heavenly Jerusalem.

NOTES

1. *Evangelical Counsels*   Also called "counsels of perfection," this term refers to Jesus' words in the Gospels counseling behavior that goes beyond the prescriptions of the Ten Commandments. The 1913 *Catholic Encyclopedia* gives this explanation: "Christ's advice is, if we would make sure of everlasting life and desire to conform ourselves perfectly to the Divine will, that we should sell our possessions and give the proceeds to others who are in need, that we should live a life of chastity for the Gospel's sake, and, finally, should not seek honours or commands, but place ourselves under obedience. These are the Evangelical Counsels, and the things which are counselled are not set forward so much as good in themselves, as in the light of means to an end and as the surest and quickest way of obtaining everlasting life." (Quoted at <http://www.newadvent.org/cathen/04435a.htm>.)

2. *Gloria Patri*   These words, meaning "Glory be to the Father," begin the traditional ending to Latin prayers. The full traditional ending in English reads, "Glory be to the Father, and to the Son, and to the Holy Spirit; as it was in the beginning, it is now, and ever shall be, world without end. Amen."

ABOUT PARACLETE PRESS

WHO WE ARE

Paraclete Press is an ecumenical publisher of books and recordings on Christian spirituality. Our publishing represents a full expression of Christian belief and practice—from Catholic to Evangelical, from Protestant to Orthodox.

Paraclete Press is the publishing arm of the Community of Jesus, an ecumenical monastic community in the Benedictine tradition. As such, we are uniquely positioned in the marketplace without connection to a large corporation and with informal relationships to many branches and denominations of faith.

We like it best when people buy our books from booksellers, our partners in successfully reaching as wide an audience as possible.

WHAT WE ARE DOING

BOOKS

Paraclete Press publishes books that show the richness and depth of what it means to be Christian. Although Benedictine spirituality is at the heart of all that we do, we publish books that reflect the Christian experience across many cultures, time periods, and houses of worship.

We publish books that nourish the vibrant life of the church and its people—books about spiritual practice, formation, history, ideas, and customs.

We have several different series of books within Paraclete Press, including the best-selling Living Library series of modernized classic texts; A Voice from the Monastery—giving voice to men and women monastics about what it means to live a spiritual life today; award-winning literary faith fiction; and books that explore Judaism and Islam and discover how these faiths inform Christian thought and practice.

RECORDINGS

From Gregorian chant to contemporary American choral works, our music recordings celebrate the richness of sacred choral music through the centuries. Paraclete is proud to distribute the recordings of the internationally acclaimed choir Gloriæ Dei Cantores, who have been praised for their "rapt and fathomless spiritual intensity" by *American Record Guide,* and the Gloriæ Dei Cantores Schola, which specializes in the study and performance of Gregorian chant. Paraclete is also the exclusive North American distributor of the recordings of the Monastic Choir of St. Peter's Abbey in Solesmes, France, long considered to be a leading authority on Gregorian chant performance.

Learn more about us at our Web site:
www.paracletepress.com
or call us toll-free at 1-800-451-5006.

OTHER PARACLETE ESSENTIALS

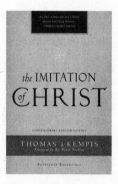

The Imitation of Christ
Thomas à Kempis
Introduction by Br. Benet Tvedten

ISBN: 978-1-55725-608-9
$15.95, 320 pages

The Imitation of Christ has enjoyed an unparalleled place in the world of books for more than five hundred years. Five thousand different editions have been published over the centuries, and it has been translated into almost every language in the world.

Why is this little book so valued? *The Imitation of Christ* transcends its era and author, having become a testament that speaks to the perennial human condition on the issues of our human relationship to God. It offers insight that is unparalleled in works before and since. The wisdom of Thomas à Kempis is for every age, for every person who seeks to live a more integrated spiritual life of seeking and finding, doing and being still.

Visit us online to see our other Classic series:
The Paraclete Giants and the *Living Library Series.*

Available from most booksellers or through Paraclete Press:
www.paracletepress.com; 1-800 451-5006.
Try your local bookstore first.